# *everyday tarot
## essentials

# *everyday tarot
## essentials

## james lynn page

## foulsham
**LONDON • NEW YORK • TORONTO • SYDNEY**

# foulsham

The Publishing House, Bennetts Close, Cippenham,
Slough, Berkshire, SL1 5AP, England

ISBN 0-572-02888-1

Printed in Great Britain by Cox & Wyman Ltd, Reading, Berkshire

# Contents

# Introduction

'*The common attitude towards Tarot, prototype of modern playing cards, is that Tarot is fortune-telling, and, therefore utterly bereft of value ... Tarot is above all a system of self-transformation.*'

Richard Roberts

Despite Richard Roberts' lofty pronouncement, it seems that many earnest seekers on the New Age path would rather stick with the fortune-telling. Indeed, it is a fascination with fortune-telling that often first impels people towards that peculiar and often beautiful set of cards known as the Tarot. Though we live in an ostensibly scientific and rational age, and 'fortune-telling' is pretty much a degraded term nowadays, the fact remains that our curiosity about our future – what lies ahead in the uncharted months, or even years, to come – remains as powerful as ever. The old attitude to fortune-telling (and one that some still maintain) was that the future could be 'told' as if it were some detailed story forming the next few chapters in our lives. In truth, however, the Tarot is not really (and arguably never has been) designed for such a purpose. In this book we will be looking at what the Tarot is really for and how its panorama of ancient and beguiling symbols works at the everyday level.

You need not have any previous experience of Tarot cards to access and use the traditional teachings here. As to what those teachings are, we might say that they cover the entire spectrum of human affairs, but they focus particularly on the development of the soul and its quest for awareness and fulfilment. The human psyche (in which the conscious and the unconscious are united) possesses a greater intention of its own – the spontaneous instinct to seek the light and unfold (like a flower) towards yet greater consciousness and growth.

However, this process involves painful experience, for it is nothing less than the life-death-rebirth cycle we find everywhere in nature – the growth of the new can only occur with the death of the old. This is also psychologically true: as we grow out of and discard old attitudes, values, emotions and opinions, we turn to something new. Inner change is a precursor for changes in our outer lives, and the connection between the two is usually not difficult to see.

Sometimes the desire for inner change comes in the form of a vague spiritual hunger – we sense that there is more to life than our material existence, something that cannot be readily encapsulated in words. This is the beginning of the 'journey within', often a difficult process, in which we work towards reconciling both the spiritual and the material aspects of life. It's a journey that we all undertake in one form or another.

In ancient myth this symbolic journey often entails situations where the hero (individual ego) must do battle with an enemy in one form or another (the 'dark side' of the unconscious). Usually, after a long and arduous struggle, the hero can at last lay claim to a precious object hitherto out of his reach: the archetypal 'buried treasure' of myth. This treasure symbolises the innate spirituality that we must find within ordinary life, and ultimately within *ourselves*. Put simply, this is the process of coming to terms with our true self.

This is also the underlying theme of alchemy, the attempt to make gold from lowly base metal – although in fact the 'gold' is really already there, waiting to be discovered beneath the dross. The inner message to which both alchemy and ancient myth allude is identical: that *nothing truly stays the same,* that we are, always, in some small sense, changing, developing and growing into *something* as we journey through life. This is the experience that the Tarot, with its use of astrological, numerological and alchemical symbolism, and its pageant of courtly figures, attempts to capture: the transformations and changes that we are all undergoing at any one time in our lives.

In the following pages you will find a comprehensive and easy-to-follow explanation of the symbolism used in the Tarot cards, including colours, shapes, objects, people and more subtle motifs. Then we will turn to what is known as the Major Arcana, which is essentially a set of 22 images that illustrate the journey towards the very centre that is our true self.

The images depicted in the Major Arcana are really personifications of the very stuff of life itself – what we might call archetypal experiences. All of us as humans have, for example, the capacity for love. This capacity is experienced differently by each individual but the basic motivation is archetypal, driven by necessity – fated, if you like. The journey of the Major Arcana is, then, an archetypal one, from the instinctual beginnings of the Fool through to the eventual fulfilment of the World. On this journey we encounter various aspects of ourselves as the greater picture unfolds. We may meet with a period when there is great change (the Wheel of Fortune), when we must make great sacrifices (the Hanged Man), when there is an ending of one of life's significant chapters (Death) or when we must face up to our darker side (The Devil). But always there is the chance to learn and move on.

Rather than seeing these events as meted out by fate, we need to ask, 'What is it within me that has attracted this event?'

If the Major Arcana captures the larger spiritual quest (new beginnings, transformation, death and rebirth), the Minor Arcana is about more everyday and less lofty experiences, which are nonetheless worthy of serious contemplation. It is to the Minor Arcana that we will be turning next. The matters dealt with in the minor suits are often of a more immediate, practical nature. You might say that they are about changes with a small 'c' – but changes that, nevertheless, can alter the course of a life to a large degree in later years. Think of any apparently insignificant decision you made at some time in the past; if you had chosen differently, your destiny today would not be the same.

We will then go on to consider how to actually use the cards – how you create a spread that will give you a formal reading: an opportunity to glimpse what the inner self is up to and where it is trying to go. If you want to think of this as 'what might happen next', fair enough, but don't forget that the true power of the Tarot is to indicate the nature of future transformations within yourself. The cards show not only what we are consciously experiencing but also the energies stored in the unconscious – which is to say, what we will soon experience.

However you use the Tarot, in order to get the right results from the cards there needs to be to be a serious and genuine desire to relate to the images, otherwise you may just be wasting your time. In short, the Tarot isn't a toy and never has been, since its first embryonic appearance way back in medieval Europe. Let's look a little, then, at the history of the cards.

# Chapter 1
# The Origins of Tarot

*'We have but little certainty who was the inventor, or who, in the first instance, developed the game, nor is that little confirmed by authority to be relied upon ... I have thus left [the answer] to be sought by the more curious.'*

Pietropaulo da San Chirico (1526)

Theories of how the Tarot developed, and from where, are many and varied. The apocryphal tales of its origins are often just as fascinating as the cards themselves. In one, they were invented in medieval China (c. 1120) in order to entertain the concubines of the reigning Emperor. In another, they were brought back from crusades to the Holy Land by the organisation of warrior-monks known as the Knights Templar, whose alleged purpose it was to guard the highways to Jerusalem. Other stories have it that the cards came from India or even Egypt. In yet another version of the Tarot's beginnings, gypsies, those former inhabitants of central Asia or North Africa, are credited with inventing the cards, despite the fact that by the time gypsies appeared in central Europe, in about the mid-fifteenth century, cards for fortune-telling were already in existence. Then there is the quaint account of the cards being made by an Indian Maharajah's wife. Exasperated by her husband's tendency to keep tugging at his long beard, she is said to have invented Tarot in order to distract him. Slightly more plausible, though just as much a product of imaginative conjecture, is the gathering of wise men in Morocco (*c.* 1200) that resulted in the development of a mysterious book of symbols, created in order to express universal truths and to overcome national language barriers. (Arguably, this is a function of the Tarot anyway!)

Moving on to the territory of verifiable fact, the first (apparent) mention scholars have found of playing cards in Europe (here referred to by the general term *naibi*) dates as far back as 1299, in Sienna. Further historical references do not appear until the late fourteenth century (usually with regard to the banning of playing cards by ecclesiastical authorities). The best known quotation regarding their early existence comes from a fifteenth-century Italian writer, Juzzo da Covelluzzo. He states that it was in 1397 that, 'the game of cards was brought to Viterbo from the country of the Saracens, where it is called *naib*'. The term *naibi*, refers to the actual figures depicted on the cards. Some writers contend that *naibi* were later used as a kind of educational system for children.

Also in fourteenth-century Italy we find the game of *tarocco*, the more complete forerunner – with its 78 cards (22 Major Arcana, 56 Minor Arcana) – of our Tarot pack. Tarocco (or *tarocchi*) is a complicated point-scoring game. Later card games tended to dispense with the Major Arcana (and in time also the Knight cards) so that we now expect a standard pack of playing cards to be only 52 in number.

If cards were alleged to have been brought from the Middle East in 1397, what is certain is that five years earlier Charles VI of France had commissioned the artist Jacquemin Gringonneur to paint the Major Arcana deck. Most of these cards survive to this day – only six are missing. These 22 major cards are called trumps, since, in the tarocco game, they are of a higher value than the remaining 56. Hence, they 'triumph' over the minor cards.

As for the number of cards in a minor suit (ten), this is supposedly based on the Indian game *dasavarata,* which illustrates the ten different incarnations of the god Vishnu, such as a tortoise, boar, dwarf, lion, axe, arrow and cow, among others.

The Tarot as we know it surfaced in late medieval Europe, in northern Italy, at a time when there was a revival of interest in what we would now call New Age subjects: magic, alchemy and astrology. Trade routes from Italy, especially sea routes, had opened up as early as the eleventh century, and in time various exotic beliefs were also part of the cargo brought back from countries east of Europe. Travellers would return with teachings from Greek myth and philosophy, from Hermetic thought or from the heresies of Egyptian gnosticism. This thirst for new and extraordinary ideas has become known as the Italian Renaissance, and reached its apotheosis in the mid-fifteenth century, by which time the nascent Tarot deck had become established.

So we have a combination of late medieval/Renaissance influences in the Tarot – from astrology (Sun, Moon, Star) to the situation at court (kings, queens, knights) through the magical arts (the Magician, Wands) to the prevailing influence of the Church (the Pope, the Devil, the Last Judgement). In this latter category Christianity's four cardinal virtues also appear in trumps such as Justice, Strength (or Fortitude), Temperance and the rather Pagan-like Hermit (once known as Prudence). Following William the Conqueror's invasion of Britain in 1066, various British mythologies, in particular those of Celtic origin, soon became known in continental Europe. By the mid-1100s, for instance, the Arthurian romances and the Grail quest stories (with their fusion of Celtic and Christian mythology) had travelled across the Channel. The sources on which the Tarot's developers could draw were therefore rich and varied. However, it would take a few hundred years for the Tarot to evolve into a deck that we would now recognise.

## Tarot packs – then and now

It is somewhat ironic that the cards were not initially used as divinatory or fortune-telling devices; it would seem that, apart from their function as mnemonic aids, their chief use was in gambling. Their ornate designs were often the indulgent conceits of rich aristocrats; indeed, some decks were so designed as to indicate the family that had commissioned their creation. For example, the Visconti pack of the early fifteenth century depicts the Visconti coat of arms somewhere on each card.

It is only really in the middle of the eighteenth century, by which time the Tarot was used exclusively for divination, that we see more obvious resemblances to modern packs. The first example of this type is the French *Tarot de Marseilles*. It is this deck, rather than its earlier forebears, from which the more standardised imagery is drawn.

### The Rider-Waite cards

The cards illustrated in this book – which would first appear in A.E. Waite's 1910 work *The Pictorial Key to the Tarot* (designed by Pamela Coleman Smith) – are likewise based on the *Tarot de Marseilles* standardisation.

Pamela Coleman Smith was a young American artist who, along with Waite, was a member of the arcane Order of the Golden Dawn. She designed and drew the pack (supposedly following Waite's instructions), which was printed by the Rider publishing company, hence this pack became known as the Rider-Waite (or Waite for short). Much of the imagery of the Rider-Waite was specially contrived for students of the occult. With its baroque, pseudo-medieval imagery, it has become one of the most popular packs with Tarot students, largely because of the picture-book effect in the Minor Arcana. Whereas in previous decks each minor card would simply show its number of 'pips' (as in the modern deck of playing cards), the Rider-Waite uses illustrative pictorial symbols. It is as if they are telling a story of their own, one that seems to progress from a particular kind of archetypal beginning through to its own conclusion. (Modern specialised packs have been able to exploit narrative structure; hence we have Tarot packs based exclusively on, say, the Arthurian legends or Greek or Norse myth, in which the minor suits relate episodes in tales of gods, heroes and heroines to the divinatory meanings of specific cards.)

The Rider-Waite made use of the magical and specifically alchemical traditions of the previous few hundred years and also anticipated the work of psychologist Carl Jung, himself intensely interested in alchemy. In the modern viewpoint, the alchemical quest to turn base metals into gold is purely metaphorical; the aim is to effect a kind of inner transformation from the leaden dross of ignorance to the majestic gold of spiritual awareness. This process, which may occur several times during one lifetime, involves a form of purification that entails the stripping away of our old self. The usual catalyst for this is a life crisis of some kind, in which our former self dies, and the self reborn is wiser, more mature, freer, transformed. The archetypal figures in the Major Arcana of the Waite pack – the Fool, the Magician, the Hanged Man, Death, the Sun – depict this process: that of the spiritual trying to become conscious in the confines of our physical bodies – the old conflict between the heavenly and the earthly.

Nearly every major card alludes to the Hermetic axiom 'as above, so below': that which is in heaven is like that which is on earth, or the greater is reflected in the lesser. This axiom also works on a subtler level in our everyday lives: for we might also say that the outer mirrors the inner, that our objective lives are largely a creation of what we are inside. Even when this is not obvious – when what happens to us is not our fault – there is often some kind of unconscious collusion on our part that has brought about a certain event. In other words, we are partly responsible for attracting situations we didn't ask for! Perhaps this is what Waite was alluding to when he wrote, 'There is a Secret Tradition concerning the Tarot, as well as a Secret Doctrine contained therein ...' But the Great Secret is a secret no longer, as I will attempt to show in the following pages.

# Chapter 2
# Inside the Tarot

In this chapter we will examine how the Tarot is constructed and look at the principles on which it is based. In short, the images are symbolic ones drawn from a rich tradition of ancient magical and religious lore, and since universal truths never change, what such symbols have to say to us is true in any age.

As I have said, the 78 Tarot cards are arranged into two *arcana* (a Latin word meaning 'mysteries'), major and minor. The 22-card Major Arcana is, as we have seen, representative of the prime archetypal journey undertaken by the soul through life; that is, the kind of major events and experiences that so often turn out be important crossroads and turning points, whether natural rites of passage or apparently fated significant events. We should always pay attention to the message when we find Major Arcana cards in our readings. Sometimes the unconscious mind is trying to communicate something that the ego may not be able to see (or perhaps just refuses to). At other times, in moments of crisis perhaps, what is happening in our life will be all too obvious and the Major Arcana cards will simply reflect what is there; however, the cards may show us how to best handle the situation.

## The four suits

The 56 minor cards (40 numbered and 16 court cards) are descendants of the game-playing packs of late medieval Europe, usually used for gambling. The suits of the Minor Arcana – Wands (or Batons), Cups (or

Chalices), Swords and Pentacles (Coins or Disks) – are recognisably the originators of the more familiar Clubs, Hearts, Spades and Diamonds of the modern playing pack. As far as their provenance goes, it is said that they signify the strata of European society in the Middle Ages. Hence, Wands for the lower classes or peasants; Cups for the clergy; Swords for the upper classes and nobility; and Pentacles for traders and merchants. But like much else in Tarot history, this explanation fails to acknowledge that the symbolism is both older and more universal than first meets the eye. The division into a four-fold scheme, for example, is hardly confined to the Tarot.

## The suits and the elements

Wands, Cups, Swords and Pentacles symbolise the four elements, considered by the Ancient Greeks to be the essential components of the universe: Fire (Wands), Water (Cups), Air (Swords) and Earth (Pentacles). The most mysterious of these elements, Fire, is not an element as such, but the ancients did not think of the elements only in the strictly objective sense that scientists do today. They defined the qualities of the elements by observing the states of matter in the world around them. Their main concern was to ascertain a thing's overall characteristics, both spiritual and physical, and so the ethereal, impalpable qualities of the elements held just as much value as their concrete ones.

Aspects of the human psyche could also be considered in terms of elemental qualities – and, indeed, today we still describe a person as 'fiery' or 'earthy'. To the ancient Greek mind, for instance, the qualities of Water could be observed in the type of person who seemed to behave like water – who was deep, reflective and adaptable on an emotional level (water assumes the shape of whatever its poured into), although sometimes (like the sea) stormy and unpredictable. The Earth type was solid, dependable and slow to act, although seemingly imbued with the wisdom of Mother Nature herself (or, if you prefer, common sense). Fire types were observed to be hot-tempered, volatile and restless, although also warm-hearted and vivacious as personalities, whereas Air types were cooler, more intellectual, and – like their element – concerned with being free to move around, in which state they functioned best.

The objects from which the Tarot suits take their name are basically tools from the magician's armoury. A consideration of how the objects themselves are used in everyday life gives us an idea as to their connection with their respective element.

The Wand can be used like a baton (indeed, in the Minor Arcana, Wands are sometimes called just that) and represents the power of its owner, hence strength and will. When lit, a Wand becomes a torch, with the power to illuminate, or to effect change. (In fact, fire itself can properly be described as a process of chemical change.)

Cups are vessels for holding liquid. Metaphorically, they indicate the way in which we contain the world of feeling; they represent our capacity for love and emotional relationships.

Swords are a cutting tool, and it is said that the logical, rational mind has a similar cutting edge. The sword's cold, sharp, reflective steel symbolises the objective mind's clear, cool logic and dispassion.

Pentacles, or disks, are material objects used in exchange for goods or services of a like value – though first they must be earned! In the Minor Arcana they speak of what we are prepared to do in order to achieve physical security, what we believe we are worth and, correspondingly, the kind of monetary wealth we are likely to acquire.

So the elements, as they relate to the four suits, are about the how the objective world is connected to the inner self. Taking a cue from the physical element, we may describe both the way a person is and what a person does, for the one follows the other. However, the Greeks were also concerned with constructing a philosophical system based on these elements, and so they defined the four chief faculties through which humankind can apprehend life: moral (Fire/Wands), aesthetic (Water/Cups), intellectual (Air/Swords) and physical (Earth/Pentacles).

## Links with Christian mythology

Leaving behind the Ancient Greeks, at some point in more recent history each of the Tarot suits became linked with a particular emblematic object from Christian mythology. Thus the Holy Grail (said to have been used to collect the drops of Christ's blood as he suffered on the cross) is connected with the suit of Cups. The Spear of Longinus, the Roman centurion who pierced Jesus's side at the Crucifixion, is connected with the suit of Wands. The Sword of the Spirit, the legendary object possessed by the Old Testament King David, is connected with the suit of Swords. And finally, the platter used at the Last Supper is connected with the suit of Pentacles.

These symbolic links were not made until many years after the compilation of the gospels. They originate from the twelfth century, the time of the Celtic Grail myths, involving King Arthur and the Knights of the Round Table.

## Celtic links

However, there is a connection with a much earlier set of symbols, the Four Treasures of Ireland, which were the gifts bestowed on humanity by a family of pre-Christian Celtic gods, the Tuatha de Danaan.

Connected with the suit of Cups is the ever-full Cauldron of Dagda (the father god). Connected with the suit of Wands is Lugh, the spear of the youthful and skilled god of the same name. Connected with the suit of Swords is the powerful and invincible sword of King Nuada. Finally, connected with the suit of Pentacles is the Stone of Sovereignty, a cube-like throne that symbolised the Earth (with its four corners) and the king's relationship to the land.

## The correspondences of the suits

The table below shows how the four Tarot suits and the four elements are classified according to the various dimensions of life. In brief we might say:

- Wands are about action and putting willpower to work in the world
- Cups are about relationships and love life
- Swords are about the development of mental strengths and how we use (or misuse) them
- Pentacles are about the capacity for acquiring money and possessions, and the channels through which these things come

| Suit | Wands | Cups | Swords | Pentacles |
|---|---|---|---|---|
| Element | Fire | Water | Air | Earth |
| Playing cards | Clubs | Hearts | Spades | Diamonds |
| Polarity | Positive | Negative | Positive | Negative |
| Faculty | Moral | Aesthetic | Intellectual | Physical |
| Human | Spirit | Soul | Mind | Body |
| Psychology | Intuition | Feeling | Thinking | Sensation |
| Plane | Etheric | Astral | Mental | Material |
| Quality | Creative | Emotional | Logical | Practical |

## What the numbers mean

If each of the minor suits represents a certain facet of the psyche or particular mode of experiencing reality, their arrangement into numerical order from one to ten adds further meanings. In this section of the book we will be looking at the significance of numbers in the Tarot and also considering how numbers relate to other symbols, such as geometric shapes and natural phenomena.

You may be wondering why I say one to ten when the Major Arcana is numbered up to 22. In fact, I could have said one to nine, because in the Chaldean system used in Western occultism, when we get to ten, we have a one and a nought (1 + 0) and so we are considered to have returned to one again. Thus there are only ever nine separate numbers. For example, card 15 (the Devil) contains the numbers 1 + 5 = 6 (The Lovers). If you look at both cards, you will see the same pair of naked lovers, indicating that these cards are related.

The number symbolism used in the Tarot derives from the mystical Jewish teaching of Kabbala, which is essentially a magical theory of creation. The study of Kabbala is really beyond the scope of this book, but the basic idea is that from the void, or negative existence, arrives a point of energy, which takes on material form and then goes through various stages of spiritual manifestation as it becomes a more complex facet of life. Though these concepts are essentially abstract, they describe how things happen (or materialise) in our lives, for thought (energy) always precedes material fact. The basic idea is best depicted geometrically: first there is the point, which then becomes a line, then a (two-dimensional) plane and finally a (three-dimensional) solid cube.

Watch out for a repeated series of particular numbers in your Tarot spreads. A recurrent number is always significant.

### Zero: unlimited potential

It might be thought that there is nothing to say about zero. How untrue! Pictorially, zero is sometimes represented by a circle, symbolising infinity, something without beginning or end. Zero's unlimited life potential can be represented by an egg, which is roughly the same shape as the figure 0 in our numerical notation system. Thus it is the cosmic egg, the womb, the Earth itself, in its role as a source of potential power and energy. Like the only unnumbered Tarot card (the Fool), zero can be placed at the end of a cycle of manifestation representing death, or at the beginning of one, where it stands for new potential, the unconscious energy that has not yet taken form.

### Ace or one: raw energy

The potential has been realised. One has a raw individual strength that can stand upright (like the figures 1 and I) and exist as an independent entity. One (like all of the aces in the Minor Arcana) is about action, the awakening of desire and the drive to assert individuality. It is also represented by the seed, the point of energy that suggests our inner essence or spirit. One represents that which is unique in us, the power to be and the power to create – just as the Magician (card number 1) does.

### Two: duality

The manifest One now becomes aware of its opposite. Two is the complement to One; it is everything its predecessor is not. If One is action, individuality and selfhood, Two is passivity, duality, compromise, reflection and the need to relate and keep things in their necessary balance. In the kabbalistic system of manifestation, the one-dimensional energy point has now become a line: that is, it has two ends. In a very simple sense, we may now say there's an awareness of polarity and opposition (either/or, north/south, inner/outer, me/you, and so on). The act of comparison has been created. It's also worth remembering that it is the line that gets us from here to there.

### Three: creativity

With Three, we see the duality (and potential conflict) of the Two resolved by an additional factor, bringing true equilibrium. What matters here is that this third factor, or harmonising aspect, results in much that is creative, life-affirming and expansive. Think of a mediator between two warring parties and the positive energy that can be released if a resolution is achieved. After the stasis of opposition there is now movement and progress. The abstract idea of Three is depicted by the equilateral triangle, for millennia a symbol of religious power, as in the Christian trinity. The triangle is the first stage of completion (or early perfection), just as in geometry it is the first perfect form that can be made using straight lines. Thus the Two (the line) begets the Three (the triangle).

### Four: form

The work of the Three is completed in the Four; if the triangle is the first perfect geometrical shape, then the square, with its four lines of equal length, is the second. Think of the four corners of the square and you already have an impression of containment, form, security. This four-square theme has long been applied to the Earth and nature: the four corners of the earth, the four winds, the four seasons and, of course, the four elements – the bricks and mortar of reality.

We might also mention the four points of the compass, pictorially represented by the cross, another emblem containing four. Crosses were used symbolically in pre-Christian religions, and occult literature speaks of the 'cross of matter', since the cross quite literally defines our physical place on Earth, pointing to what is above and below us, and what is to our left and right (while we are at its exact centre). Hence the cross is just another way of representing the idea of the square – a complete and self-contained system, referring specifically to life on earth (as opposed to the spirit). Thus Four represents matter, form, order, solidity and the physical limitations of human life.

## Five: change

Where the stability and security of the Four must mean stasis (since no future growth can occur), the Five stirs things up in order for there to be new development. When the form of the Four breaks down, the energy released must seek new channels, so for a while there is instability. This is why all of the Minor Arcana Fives have such negative connotations. It seems as if we are experiencing the destruction of what has happened in the Fours, but such changes are necessary to human consciousness and its growth. It is no accident that Five is the number of the human being, its geometric shape, the Pentacle, representing the figure of a person with arms and legs fully outstretched. As human beings we also have five senses, five fingers and five toes. Five is also about our relationship to the rest of the universe, and the limitations (or struggles) we may face each time we act upon our environment. It is about the striving for conscious awareness, which finally gives way to the light and wisdom of experience.

## Six: balance

Six represents equilibrium and is a stabilising factor after the upheaval of the Five. There is strength through harmony here and an awareness of the correct relationship of one thing to another. In other words, our life now seems to be in proportion and proper balance. The Six's function is suggested beautifully by the related geometric symbol of the hexagram, the six-pointed star that became Judaism's Star of David. The figure is composed of two interlocking triangles, one upright and the other inverted. The upright triangle is the magical symbol for Fire (the rising spirit, consciousness) while the downward-pointing triangle represents water (the descent of the soul, the unconscious). This construction, then, is of a perfect union of opposites, containing both aspects of the human (questing spirit and reflective soul) necessary to the whole.

## Seven: transition

Seven has been described by one authority as 'temporary cessation' (as in 'on the seventh day God rested'). Seven is traditionally the number of the mystic. The ancient Greek mathematicians noticed that it was the only integer that couldn't be divided evenly into the 360-degree circle. Thus it became imbued with mysterious, even divine, qualities. If Five is the number of the human being, Seven represents the cosmic beauty of humanity; if Five is about the efforts of the individual, Seven represents the splendour of God's handiwork.

Each of the different phases of the lunar cycle takes seven days to complete and, before the invention of powerful modern telescopes, only seven planets could be seen in the night sky. For Pythagoras, the movement of these planets resulted in the 'music of the spheres', which was created by the basic seven notes of the diatonic scale. The rainbow also contains seven colours.

In practical terms, Seven represents an awareness of the infinite, or the spiritual – the unconscious forces that shape our lives. It allows a sense of larger meaning beyond the ego. As we move on from the Six to gain a more profound awareness of Life, Seven tells us that individual willpower has little place in the world now, that we must trust in the larger picture and rely on intuition, inner guidance and contemplation of the spirit. The geometric forms symbolising the seven are the triangle (three) over the square (four) signifying the dominance of spirit over matter. The transition alluded to in this number's key word is, then, the movement from one phase of life to another as we wait to be spiritually reborn.

## Eight: materialisation

From the rather abstruse concepts of the Seven comes the physical manifestation of the Eight. If there has been cessation of real activity in the Seven, here is both movement and materialisation. The idea of movement is expressed in the shape of the numeral itself – the symbol for infinity and the working out of a certain cycle of events that will one day repeat themselves. This glyph appears in both the Magician and the Strength card, the latter also being number eight of the Major Arcana. The theme of materialisation is aptly shown in the related geometric symbol of the cube. It is the square squared, the basic four-sided (two-dimensional) shape given the extra dimension of depth. Also alluded to here is the fact that within the structure of matter (our bodies and the physical world), the process of renewal and recycling is always going on. Nothing ever stays the same; the outer form changes, grows old and dies, while the spirit moves on and reincarnates.

### Nine: completion

Another specialised number (like the Seven), Nine represents final attainment, the true end of a cycle, wholeness, totality, perfection and completion. It is the highest individual number (ten being a combination of one and nought.) However, something interesting happens when any whole number is added to, or multiplied by, nine; either the nine disappears or it 'absorbs' the other number. The Ancients must have been pleasantly startled to find that if, say, $5 + 9 = 14$, then $1 + 4$ takes us back to 5. Alternatively, if $5 \times 9 = 45$, then $4 + 5 = 9$. It is as if the Nine wilfully conceals itself; or is it the One that is doing the concealing?

Since Nine can in certain instances 'contain' all the other single numbers, it is associated with wisdom and occult knowledge. The word 'occult' literally means 'hidden', and Nine is a hidden presence if we use the number reduction technique with the Major Arcana. Let's take the Devil again, for instance – Trump 15. As we have seen, $1 + 5 = 6$, which is the Lovers, and we've noted that these two cards are related. But the difference between 15 and 6 is, of course, 9. (This bit of arithmetic works with all the Major Arcana cards, so that all those separated by nine are secretly related.) In other words, Nine unifies everything; it is the secret thread connecting all of reality.

### Ten: rebirth

With Ten we go back to One and start again. Ten is simply the renewal of a cycle, or an elevation on to a higher plane of that cycle, so that instead of our lives merely moving around in circles, we ascend a little higher with each revolution. Thus Ten might better be described as a spiral. Card number 10 in the Major Arcana, the Wheel of Fortune, is about new beginnings, a fresh turn in the cycle of life, and is quite often equated with the opportunity to learn from past mistakes. Again, the Wheel is really a spiral, for we can go down just as easily as up; it all depends on how we act.

Of course, the idea of rebirth and renewal implies the end of a previous phase, and the Tens in the Minor Arcana, when considered in combination with the meaning of each individual suit, show how endings and beginnings work themselves out. For example, the physical substances of water (Cups) and earth (Pentacles) are more self-sustaining and enduring than fire (Wands) or air (swords). Thus the Ten of Cups and the Ten of Pentacles have a far more congenial divinatory meaning than the Ten of Wands or the Ten of Swords, as Wands and Swords cannot renew or sustain themselves.

## Colours

Below is a list of the keywords associated with each of the colours used symbolically in the Waite Tarot for both the Major and the Minor Arcana. With a little practice you will soon be able to see for yourself why certain colours are used. There is often a dominant background colour that symbolises the overriding theme of the card. For example, the Magician is set against backdrop of yellow, the colour of conscious awareness, something to which he aspires. He wears a red cloak and white tunic – red for will in action and white for spiritual awareness.

**White:** Purity, spirituality, clarity, healing, wholeness.
**Yellow:** The light of awareness, the conscious mind, intellect, rational thought.

**Blue/turquoise:** The soul, feelings and emotions, thoughts driven by the intuitive and poetic side of our nature – or, simply, non-rational thoughts.

**Green:** Fertility, nature, growth, human instinct, materialisation in the concrete world.

**Red:** The spirit, active will, life-force, dynamic energy (which causes change).

**Purple:** Wisdom, understanding, occult or hidden knowledge (often hinted at in cards where this colour is prominent).

**Black:** The unconscious, introversion, negation, inversion, solemnity. (In some cards, black has been added to background colours to suggest the intermixture of a tendency towards 'blackness' and all of its meanings.)

## Masculine and feminine

The basic natural duality of masculine and feminine is at the very heart of magical philosophy. These terms are not to be confused with the traits of actual men and women themselves; real people contain a mixture of both masculine and feminine characteristics – there are just as many dynamic women as there are passive men. As used by occult philosophers, masculine and feminine are archetypal references, applicable to all kinds of phenomena in the world. The masculine elements are Fire and Air (they are active, dynamic, and giving), and the feminine elements are Earth and Water (they are passive and static, and they absorb and receive). This very simple division into active masculine and passive feminine in turn entails other subtler features in the Tarot. We will be considering some of these below.

### Male and female

Where a male figure is depicted on a card, the principle represented is outgoing, action-oriented and concerned with differentiation (what makes 'this' distinct from 'that'). Males in the Tarot are about initiative, innovation and change, or they symbolise worldly, paternal authority. (The Hanged Man is a exception here, because he is symbolically inverted, so the normal masculine values are turned upside-down.)

Cards depicting a female figure represent that which is reflective and inward-looking, with the ability to see intuitively the whole picture (or both sides of it), to harmonise and to compromise, and to relate to and enjoy the present for what it is. If the male is about innovation, the female stabilises and secures or capitalises on what is already there. One of the most vital facets of the feminine is the ability to get in touch with aspects of the inner self that are in conflict, and thus to accept and live with oneself fully.

## Left and right, above and below

This feature of orientation in space is often overlooked in explorations of the Tarot, though the briefest inspection will tell you that it is significant in the cards. Take a look at either the Major or the Minor Arcana and notice what the human figures are doing with either their left or their right hand. Observe which direction they are facing, and note whether there is symmetry between the left and right sides of the image. It will become clear that these details are far from irrelevant.

In short, the right-hand side belongs to the archetypal masculine set of values described above. It represents the conscious mind, logic, will, the exterior surface and what you make happen. It is about giving out, and what is active, rational and looking outwards to the world. The left-hand side belongs to the feminine. It is what is in the unconscious, the inner depths, the feelings and the subjective experience of what happens to you. It is passive, and is concerned with receiving, intuiting and looking inwards to the self.

To see how this works out in practice, compare the Ace of Cups and the Ace of Swords – each rather different from the other in meaning. The soul qualities and surge of feeling in the Ace of Cups are not only represented by the suit, for the cup is held in the receptive left hand. In the Ace of Swords, the new intellectual and mental powers symbolised by the number and the suit are reinforced by the fact that the Sword is held in the dynamic right hand. In the Major Arcana, swords and magic wands are quite often held in the right hand, since these objects symbolise change, power and innovation.

Look at the Magician's gesture in card 1: his right hand points to the heavens and his left hand towards earth, symbolising the maxim 'as above so below'. This gesture expresses the universal truth that what is up (or out) there is mirrored by what is down (or in) here – thus heaven and earth, world and self, matter and mind. At the same time, this is also a symmetry that we should always be aiming for in our lives – in other words, an integration of and a healthy balance between our outer physical circumstances and our inner spiritual self.

As if to emphasis this idea, the heaven/earth motif is repeated several more times in the Major Arcana, most obviously in cards 5, 6, 11 and 15, and also more subtly in cards 3, 4 and 14. In fact, the theme of the spiritual or celestial being secretly connected to earthly, human sphere is present in virtually all of the Major Arcana cards. They often depict cosmic phenomena occurring in the sky juxtaposed with human beings or animals below. You might like to study these images more carefully and then meditate on their possible meanings.

Other pictorial symbols to look for are streams and pools. Wherever these are depicted, hidden (watery) depths are present in some form. Hilltops and mountains (notably seen in Strength and the Hermit) stand for the lofty heights of the rational mind and the ways in which it can detach itself from the mundane affairs of ordinary mortals. Whichever card they appear on, the implication is that some part of our journey will lift us out of the ordinary, or we must make the effort to raise ourselves above our present experience in order to obtain a clear overall view.

## The court cards

The 16 court cards comprise four of each suit, representing Page, Knight, Queen and King. Their modern descendants can be seen in the Knave, Queen and King of the modern playing deck. It seems that as playing cards grew in popularity in Renaissance Europe, either the Knight (or in some cases the Queen) was jettisoned. This has left us with the 52 playing cards we are familiar with today, as opposed to the 56 of the Minor Arcana.

The court cards in the Tarot are personifications of each suit; they embody the human characteristics, if you like, of their respective element. In the past, the appearance of one of these figures in a spread was interpreted in a very literal way: the Queen of Cups meant that you would meet a dark, mysterious, sexy woman; and the King of Pentacles meant that you would marry a rich, older man. But we take a more holistic view these days and tend to interpret the court cards from a psychological perspective. Like the figures who populate our night-time dreams, they are qualities and traits brought to life in a representative human form, and we should not mistake the outer figure for the underlying energy or principle it symbolises.

This understanding is at the heart of all symbolism of course, yet it is easy to mistake outer garb for inner reality with the court cards. To return to the Queen of Cups for example, her appearance in a spread may mean that the qualities she represents are central to a certain relationship issue at present. It is certainly possible that a Queen of Cups type of woman may have entered your life, but it is equally possible that (regardless of your gender) her traits are present in you, and the Tarot is calling attention to the fact. As we have seen, masculine and feminine are universal principles. If a male querent (the person asking the question) gets the Queen of Cups in a reading, he could be encountering the deeper, more intensely emotional and perhaps irrational side of himself. Always bear in mind that the court cards, while referring to human characteristics, are not to be interpreted solely on the basis of their literal gender.

## Pages

The Pages represent the embryonic and fragile stage in the development of a particular suit. Here, it is early days; there is much ahead and much to do. There may be a vague sense of the possibilities associated with the respective suit, but things have hardly begun to get going, and thus patience and care are required. Traditionally representing a young person, either male or female, the Page's natural place in the Minor Arcana sequence is after the ten – thus number 11, which reduces to 2 (1 + 1 = 2) symbolising the need to relate and understand. The appearance of a Page in a spread almost always signifies the need to be receptive to incipient changes that will take time to develop.

## Knights

Knights stand for the principle of communication and movement; being able to move swiftly upon their mounts, they represent the speed with which ideas and knowledge can be absorbed and disseminated. They are about youthful vigour and rapid change, and can adapt to just about any situation. Like the air, they require freedom of movement. Astrologically, they relate broadly to the mutable signs Gemini (Swords), Virgo (Pentacles), Sagittarius (Wands) and Pisces (Cups). They are traditionally associated with young male adults. The Knight's place in the Minor Arcana suits is number 12, which reduces to 3 (1 + 2 = 3). Three stands for creativity, communication and a sense of things being on the move.

## Queens

Queens are the embodiment of stability, solidity and dependability. They seldom change and are slow to do so, yet they do develop their innate qualities – those connected with the suit – in a thorough manner and focus on their objectives more carefully than the Knights. They represent the archetypal feminine qualities of receptivity, patience and gentle understanding, though they cannot be persuaded to adapt like the Knights; all of them are immovable once they have made up their mind. In astrology, they relate broadly to the fixed signs Taurus (Pentacles), Leo (Wands), Scorpio (Cups) and Aquarius (Swords). They are traditionally associated with mature women. The Queen's place in the Minor Arcana sequence is number 13, which reduces to 4 (1 + 3 = 4), representing the stability and enduring nature of the Earth. All the Queens, irrespective of suit, have this rock-like reliability.

## Kings

The Kings represent all that is authoritative, controlling, worldly and powerful, and are associated with a stage in life that has the wisdom of experience behind it. With the archetypal masculine comes leadership and the ability to take the initiative and get new projects underway, organising others and generally being in charge. The Kings all have this pioneering, forward-looking vision. Never content with what is, they must always seek to improve things or create anew. Astrologically, they relate broadly to the cardinal signs Aries (Wands), Cancer (Cups), Libra (Swords) and Capricorn (Pentacles). They are traditionally associated with mature men. The King's place in the minor suit is number 14, which reduces to 5 (1 + 4 = 5), symbolising change, fresh initiative and new energies that dispense with old forms and previous situations.

# Chapter 3
# How the Tarot Works

et's return to a question I touched upon in the introduction: can the Tarot predict the future? The short answer would have to be yes, but only if we qualify the phrase 'predict the future'.

First of all, let's look at what we are actually trying to do with a Tarot spread. If we begin, in a rather starry-eyed way, by expecting the Tarot to foretell our future, we are assuming that the future is already formed in some way in a complete package. The consequence of this assumption is that we can do nothing about what the future holds. Although some people do apparently believe that life, or destiny, is something that happens to us as we stand by like powerless observers, this is certainly not my attitude, and nor is it the attitude of any experienced Tarot reader I know of.

Then there is the contrary school of thought that says we can make just about whatever we want of our lives, that circumstances can be changed by our own will almost any time we choose and that even the most dire Tarot reading is 'only psychological'. I don't wholly go along with this attitude either. To effect any useful and meaningful change in our life usually requires time, effort and patience, and if we end up with several 'bad' cards in a reading they cannot be rationalised away. The point is, they are there because *we helped to put them there*. In other words (and if they don't refer to some obvious current pitfall), they are reflecting something deep within us, something significant about ourselves.

So the future, being merely an extension of the present moment, is really what we have been (perhaps unwittingly) creating all along. One event always follows as a reaction to a previous one. We can see this (if we have the time and the patience) by tracing all the major changes in our life back as far as we can remember. Events do not so much happen to us as we happen to them, and so what we call the future is nothing more than the outworking of the eternal present moment – a concept well-known to Zen Buddhists.

What may be a new concept to some, however, is the fact that the present moment is not simply a point in time but, as it relates to the individual, something with a dynamic and a particular quality of its own. Those familiar with the practice of biorhythms (in which an individual's highs and lows are measured and recorded in order to work out their own personal mood and performance cycle) will know about the phenomenon of a moment in time having characteristics particular to the individual. Astrologers are also well aware of this personal life-cycle – that a certain period in a person's existence, as a certain planet crosses a sensitive point in their chart, will be a good time for them to work out or express a particular energy configuration. But whether this is experienced as an outer or inner event, the energy for it comes from the individual.

The dynamics behind Tarot readings are not that different, except that in the case of the Tarot we have symbolic cards as opposed to planets. You may be wondering how a pack of cards could be powerful enough to predict such significant moments and the energies they contain. As a Tarot student once said to me, they are, after all, nothing more than printed images on a piece of card. The short answer is that we do not know, any more than we know why (as quantum physics indisputably shows) the human mind is inextricably related to the world of matter.

We do know that the mechanism of the unconscious reaches out into the larger, objective world and somehow acts upon it, and that there are often uncanny coincidences at work far too poignant for words. Such encounters with 'fate' evoke such a sense of the familiar that it can seem as if the environment itself is responding to us, and us alone. Time and again we hear of something happening at just the right moment for the individual, perhaps because it heralds their next step on the path of destiny. Perhaps Tarot spreads can be considered as a momentary snapshot of that unfolding destiny.

But destiny has not been carved in stone for all time; it is subject to change. The trajectory of a missile can be estimated over a certain distance and at a certain speed; however, the missile will end up at a very different target with a slight change of position when it is fired. In other words, by changing the present a little, we can alter the future a great deal.

## Approaching a Tarot reading

Before we shuffle the cards, we need to consider the issue of whether it is right to read for oneself. Unfortunately, if you are really to learn – which is to say, to understand the symbolic images in terms of your own experience – there is really no other way.

The general objection to reading your own cards stems from the quite reasonable idea that you are very likely to try to make the meaning fit yourself in the most flattering way, and when cards appear to have a negative connotation, you may gloss over them in some sense. You can avoid this natural tendency of the ego if you are able to go beyond the notion of 'good' and 'bad' cards. 'Good' and 'bad' cards reflect what is, after all, only part of a greater picture. Whatever card appears in our spread – whether it portends difficulties or just a good time socially – it always brings information we can learn from. If you approach the cards as a mirror, the spread is you looking back at yourself.

If you are able to work on the Tarot with a friend, then perhaps their objectivity can help to distance you from your own image and you can learn to read the cards without reading into them what you want to see.

As I have already mentioned, you should approach the cards seriously, with a genuine desire to relate to them. There's a very good practical reason for this, too: the more sincere the attitude to the cards, the better the results! Call it the mind–matter continuum or just the way the cards behave, but this connection between yourself and the Tarot will get increasingly uncanny as your relationship develops. And then there is the matter of how you treat the cards. Whether you enjoy your deck for its pure aesthetic value or consider it to be a practical part of your of occult toolkit is up to you. There is a tradition of storing cards inside a silken wrap or a wooden box in order to protect their 'vibrations', but whether you choose to do this is entirely up to you. Wherever you keep your cards, you would be well advised to treat them seriously once they are in a spread.

The time period covered by a reading mostly depends on the matter on which you are seeking advice. If yours is a simple and direct question, the time period in the answer will probably cover anything from the next few days to the next few weeks. When it comes to a more generalised reading – one that covers various aspects in your life in an overall and integrated way – a rule-of-thumb time period of about six months is given by some writers.

A word of warning: don't fall into the habit of consulting the cards on an almost daily basis to see what they have in store for you (a typical temptation for the student), as they will almost certainly start to play tricks on you!

## Reversed cards

At this point, it would be useful to include a few words about reversed cards – cards that become inverted during shuffling. There are Tarot readers who argue that when a card is reversed in this way, its meaning is altered; however, this is not a line I take. Some Tarot readers argue that the meaning of a reversed card is just that – the opposite of what is stated as its traditional interpretation. Others argue that a reversed card represents an exaggeration or misuse of the upright card's qualities. To me, this all seems rather arbitrary and also unnecessarily complex.

The core idea behind these different ways of reading reversed cards seems to be that such a card has overtones of negativity, as if its true expression has been corrupted in some way. But this attitude is a hangover from the late medieval period when the Tarot's archetypes were developed. In those days, card orientations were two-dimensionally either good or bad, and that was that. If an individual had cards falling in a reversed position, all kinds of dreadful events would be predicted.

While some still take this black and white view of the cards, I agree with Liz Greene and Juliet Sharman Burke (authors of the *Mythic Tarot*), who point out that 'each card contains within it a dark and light dimension'. In other words, as we have already noted, the cards are not to be interpreted in a flat good or bad sense. In the former case, too much of a good thing will eventually bring boredom, and in the latter case, we often gain valuable life lessons from so-called negative experiences. We also have to look at each card within the context of the overall spread – what are the surrounding cards and who exactly is the reading for? In other words, the age, sex and personal circumstances of the querent are relevant.

Today's Tarot readers are a little more sophisticated than their medieval forerunners, and most do not think about the cards in terms of omens. We generally prefer the term 'divination' to 'cartomancy' or 'fortune-telling by cards', because it more accurately reflects the way that we think about our relationship to the rest of the universe – by which the cards do not foretell a fixed set of events. Most people's lives do not run along static and perfectly predictable lines; in other words, they are dynamic and subject to change. If the cards reflect our lives, then they must also reflect that quality of movement, change and dynamism. Divination by Tarot suggests a glimpse of the overall psyche, of the inner and outer world of the individual and the direction in which it is moving – or better still, unfolding – whether we see this in terms of psychological or of literal, concrete events.

## A simple three-card spread

There is usually no better teacher than experience, so let's get started. We will look at some of the more elaborate and complex ways of laying out the cards later in the book; for now we're going to use a simple format that will give you an idea of how to use the spread itself and a sense of the way in which certain cards combine. This three-card spread is laid out in a horizontal line, the cards representing, from left to right, past, present and future (though it's worth noting that past, present and future are not the only divisions that this simple spread can be used with). Some Tarot readers add a fourth card, but the three-card spread works well enough and is an excellent starting point.

First of all, shuffle the cards thoroughly, as you should before every reading. Next, either spread them out on a flat surface or make them into a fan. Then, at random, pick out three cards and place them face-down in a pile. Turn over the first card (the top one) and place it in the centre in front of you; this represents the present. Turn over the second card and place it to the left of the first; this represents the past. Turn over the third card and place it on the right of the first; this represents the future.

A little reflection will tell you that out of the three cards it is the one representing the present that is the key to everything. In the present, the past still has its traces and continues to make itself felt, while the future is going to be affected in one way or another by what happens in the present.

Let's suppose that your cards are:

*Past*

*Present*

*Future*

1 **The present:** The Lovers.
2 **The past:** The Fool.
3 **The future:** The Eight of Pentacles.

You can now look up the meanings of these cards on pages 50, 62 and 151.

A basic interpretation of this spread might be along these lines. The card for the past, the Fool, indicates that your instinct and readiness for the new and untried has led you into a situation where you have to make an important choice between two attractive alternatives, represented by the present card, the Lovers. The future card, the Eight of Pentacles, shows that the likely outcome of whatever you decide will mean embarking upon the development of new skills and work methods pertaining to a certain goal.

Let's say that you are in a job where you have been feeling hemmed in, and you are thirsting for something new (the Fool). Here, of course, the past is still impinging on the future, but the desire for fresh fields is so strong that you know a decision will be called for sooner or later (the Lovers). Then, in time, perhaps you will decide to undertake a new course of study (the Eight of Pentacles) that will facilitate a job change.

There will always be something in your everyday existence that the cards relate to, and in some instances it will be pretty obvious what. But the reading should also come about in an organic way, without you trying to make anything fit. Let the cards speak to you first and foremost through their images. How do they feel to you? Some cards may not yield their meaning straight away, so be patient. Can you detect something other than the obvious being hinted at? In the final analysis, the real skill of Tarot reading lies in being able to synthesise the cards in a meaningful and realistic way.

## Using one card to ask a question

Asking a direct question of the Tarot is one of the more interesting ways to use it. For this you need only select one card after you have shuffled the pack, though you can, if you wish, add other cards to the answer to elaborate the meaning. You can ask any kind of question, but be aware that the answer you get may not be a simple yes or no. Although it is obvious that certain cards have a generally positive ring about them while others seem rather gloomy (take a look at the Three of Swords, for example), in other cases this isn't so clear-cut, and working out whether your answer is a positive or a negative may take some thought. The real skill in this – and it is one you will be developing as you work with the Tarot – rests in forming a correct and sincere relationship to the cards. This involves a willingness to search and explore.

Again, I must stress that there is in fact no such thing as good and bad cards. I mentioned the Three of Swords above, considered by some to be one of the worst you can overturn. But, like all the cards, the Three of Swords needs to be understood in the context of the whole reading. If it really does seem to be reflecting a painful situation, try to make friends with it. Do some soul-searching and ask yourself why this particular card has appeared. Be prepared for some genuine self-honesty – just what is it that you appear to be getting wrong? How much have you yourself really contributed to this situation – perhaps through fear or ignorance? In most cases, the answer will be obvious.

### The Tarot and the *I Ching*

Sometimes an answer provided by a single card can take you off in a different direction and get you thinking about the issue in a different way. Often this leads to the profoundest of conclusions. In this sense, asking a particular card to yield an answer of sorts (which often turns out to be an obtuse one at that) is in keeping with divination by the ancient Chinese book of wisdom the *I Ching*.

In brief, the *I Ching*, or *Book of Changes*, is a divinatory text based on the formation of 64 hexagrams, themselves created from two combined trigrams. These two trigrams are essentially made up of either whole or broken lines, and represent the manifestations of masculine and feminine forces in the universe (yang and yin) combined with various phenomena found in nature. You arrive at your own particular hexagram (its six lines) by a process of throwing coins or arranging yarrow stalks, and it is then a simple matter to look up your hexagram in the book and meditate on the advice given. The reading will be relevant for you as an individual at that particular moment in time.

In his English translation of the *I Ching*, John Blofeld mentions the need for absolute sincerity when forming a question, lest you encounter the *I Ching's* 'disconcerting but humorous means of rejecting questions that are improper in themselves or put to it in improper circumstances'. And the Tarot works in pretty much the same way; in giving you your answer, it will always direct you to the heart of the question itself.

### Shall I change my job?

Let's now ask the Tarot a direct question, for example: 'Shall I change my job?' And let's imagine that the answer is the Eight of Pentacles. As you can see, this is no simple yea or nay; the Tarot is effectively saying, 'If you are going to change jobs, the new one will require that you learn new skills', and this may well be something you hadn't thought of. The

Eight of Pentacles is known as the apprentice card and is related to the development of new energies directed towards material ends, where labour is about to lead to reward. You could, though, in this example, expand the general meaning of the answer; the card could be saying, for instance, that you may have to bring about a change of attitude towards work and life as a whole if things are going to be a success. Here, the necessary work could be on an inner level – encountering yourself anew, realising the need for inner change and relinquishing old habit patterns.

## Will my house move turn out well?

Let's now consider another example of using a single card in an oracular fashion to answer a fairly simple question. A client of mine had already set in motion the process of moving house and wanted some kind of confirmation that all would be well. She phrased the question as: 'How will my recent decision to move house work out?' She was already looking forward to the move with keen anticipation; this was to be a fresh start in beautiful surroundings with a new phase of guaranteed financial security. The card she selected as her answer was, to her great surprise, the Five of Cups, traditionally associated with emotional loss, sorrow and feelings of depression. It is the card where the cup of love, or joy, is overturned. My client was perplexed to know just why this particular card chose her.

When we discussed the issue before her move, I was certain I knew why this card had appeared, but I advised her to come back for another reading three months after she had settled into the new house. When, after the three months had passed, we met again, I told her I knew that the house move was going to be beneficial, and then I asked her whether there was any regret or sadness mixed in with her new-found joy. She told me that although the new house was 'absolutely wonderful', she was surprised to find herself experiencing huge pangs of nostalgia (accompanied by tears) for her old place. Although not always ideal, it had been her home for ten years; she hadn't realised just how emotionally attached she had become to it. As the Five of Cups predicted, she was now grieving its loss.

## Unexpected answers

This kind of surprise answer – the one that somehow throws you off guard – is actually a common experience. Generally speaking, we would probably assume that getting a better home would be a cause for elation, and in this case that was broadly true, but our objective situation is not our whole situation. The sorrowful Five of Cups was a reminder to this woman that our inner selves – containing our memories and our emotional lives – need attention too. It was basically saying, 'You need to pay attention to your deepest feelings; here there is loss, no matter how fulfilled you feel in your present situation.' In the broader context of this woman's life it was also saying, 'This reaction, though confusing, is entirely natural. You have just given up a symbol of security, something to which you have been attached for many years; of course there is a sense of pain. The fact that that you have just begun a new chapter in life has not yet properly registered with your innermost emotions.' And so, through reflecting back what was most real within this individual, the Tarot helped her to learn something about her inner self and about her own emotional mechanisms. This is one of the ways in which the Tarot is invaluable – it teaches us about ourselves.

# Chapter 4
# The Greater Mysteries –
# the Major Arcana

As we have said, the Major Arcana is made up of 22 cards and the word *arcana* actually means 'mysteries'. These cards are sometimes used alone in readings, especially when the questioner is looking for answers relating to their inner self. The cards are based on archetypes of human beings, essential forms of human states. In this chapter, we are going to examine them individually and look in some detail at how they can be read.

## 0 The Fool

Beneath a setting sun, a brightly dressed young man is apparently about to step over the edge of a precipice, while his white dog warns of the impending fall. The Fool holds a white flower lightly in his left hand; in his right he carries a knapsack on the end of a wooden pole. His garments are a cap and feather, and a tunic that on the outside is bright green and decorated with spirals, and on the inside red.

THE FOOL.

The unnumbered card '0' symbolises that which is without beginning or end – a cycle of endlessly repeating events – and might perhaps more properly be placed at the end of the Major Arcana since it signifies a descent of sorts before we emerge into a new life once more. But it all depends on how you look at it, for the Fool represents both end and beginning, or rather a kind of limbo in between where things remain in suspension. All is pure potential here, and a journey into the unknown is indicated. It's up to us to have the courage to take that first small step – every long journey, as the proverb says, begins with this.

This card is full of colour symbolism. The reds, whites and greens are the colours of alchemy. The white stands for the Fool's pure spirit, his young soul ready to seek out new adventure; the green is the colour of initiation and the ripening of self-awareness; while the red symbolises incipient wisdom and maturity –

perhaps the Fool doesn't really need his dog's warning. However, the wisdom that the fool possesses is not the conventional sort. The case for having the Fool at the end of the Major Arcana rests on the fact that he has, in fact, passed through all the lessons of the preceding 21 cards and is now totally free. He has the wisdom of the fool; that is, he has witnessed the follies of humans, one of the greatest of which is to resist the forces of change.

In our everyday lives we often erect our defences and insist on remaining secure – emotionally and materially – sometimes to the point where our lives are so habit-bound and repetitive that we are barely living at all. The Fool is free from all of this – look how lightly he travels. He has learned that to be able to live in the moment, to enjoy the ever-changing 'now', is the greatest freedom and joy we can ever know. He is ready to undertake any new journey unencumbered by the past, for in a sense he doesn't have one. He thus inhabits the eternal present. He has learned the art of living, of being fully alive to each moment, and this is why he is truly wise: he is psychologically free. In the physical world his sense of airy detachment and recklessness may make him seem like the greatest fool, but he knows better.

When this card appears in a spread, it is an indication that anything is possible. We may be about to take a step into the unknown and should try to follow our instincts rather than being constrained by conventional advice or logic.

**Key words for interpretation:** A necessary step into the unknown; the start or end of a cycle; heedless actions with positive or negative consequences; instinct; freedom.

# 1 The Magician

A young, red-robed man raises a wand heavenwards with his right arm, while his left points to earth. Above his head is the figure eight, or lemniscate, an emblem of completeness or eternity. This idea is echoed in the belt at his waist, which resembles the ourobouros – the serpent that eats its own tail. On a table before him the four elements are represented by a wand, a cup, a sword and a pentacle, while lilies and roses (symbols of death and life respectively) grow at his feet.

The first card proper of the Major Arcana stands for raising consciousness, the process of self-realisation, of discovering who and what we really are. As such it represents the dynamic of the Tarot itself. Whether we know it or not, the psyche is constantly unfolding towards greater awareness, both of the outside world and of itself.

The 'as above, so below' gesture made by the Magician indicates that whatever qualities are perceived out there in the universe are always a reflection of what is within. Other ways of expressing this truth include 'on earth, as it is in heaven' and 'like attracts like'. According to this basic occult premise, there is no real difference between the observer and the observed, between you and the universe, for both are intimately related at a deeper level. Any Magician worth their salt knows this, and thus seeks to understand who and what they themselves are. The tools for such perception are the wand (intuition), the cup (emotions), the sword (intellect) and the pentacle (physical senses).

The white wand pointing upwards stands for the Magician's higher will, with which he seeks to harness the energies of the universe and direct them towards his own ends, spiritual or material. In a sense this higher will (also called simply spirit, or pure consciousness) is the overall animating force in human beings; it is what makes them want to live in the first instance. The Magician represents the desire on the part of the greater psyche to become self-aware, to undertake the great quest for knowledge and wisdom. From the individual ego's point of view, the quest always leads back to the self. It is thus cyclical, hence the figure eight above the Magician's head, and the hints of beginnings (roses for life) and endings (lilies for death) in the flower symbolism.

THE MAGICIAN.

If the Fool is all instinct, then the Magician has developed mental powers and an increased self-awareness to lead him along the path. Here, there is a dawning sense of the new together with the clear insight and power of initiative that is likely to end in success.

When this card appears in a spread, the message is to have confidence in ourselves and use our own inner strengths to make the changes we desire. It indicates that we have the energy and power to be in control.

**Key words for interpretation:** Self-knowledge and willpower, and the means to use them cleverly and skilfully; manipulation; adaptability; insight; clarity; self-confidence.

## 2 The High Priestess

A priestess in white and blue garments sits between two pillars of wisdom, one black, one white, with the Torah scrolled up in her lap. A veil behind her is decorated with fruits, while a crescent moon sits at her feet.

THE HIGH PRIESTESS

In a way, the High Priestess is the complement of the Magician (which is why she appears as the next card); if the Magician is concerned with the skilful exercise of the will and the powers of conscious initiation, the High Priestess governs the realm of the unconscious, its hidden matters, and that inner voice to which we must listen attentively and carefully. It has been said by occultists and psychologists alike that the unconscious possesses a kind of 'absolute knowledge' (in the words of Jung). It seems to work in an almost omniscient way, containing the outline of our future. The High Priestess is a personification of this knowing place deep within us. Just as the Magician embodies the conscious and successful application of the will, she embodies that which guides and inspires, that which lies behind the outer self, and which can only be accessed by a trusting faith and a genuine desire to understand on the part of the ego.

The High Priestess is best exemplified in our experience of nocturnal dreams, those manifestations of the unconscious as strong feelings and often strange images. Dreams, on the whole, are a kind of reflection (albeit in an often confusingly symbolic form) of our conscious lives, of all our hopes, values, desires, beliefs and so on. Some dreams are inspirational. They act as a kind of guide, dropping hints as to what step we ought to take next in our lives. Some – rare – dreams actually do predict future events; others act as emotional compensations – we dream of having our fantasies fulfilled simply because they are never going to be realised in our waking lives. All of this dream activity seems to add up to some specialised unconscious knowledge, of which the High Priestess is the embodiment.

The High Priestess sits between the twin pillars of Boaz and Jachin (the poles of dark and light, archetypal feminine and masculine) because in truth she belongs to neither; rather she is the bridge between them, guarding the entrance to mystery of life itself. Expressed more simply, she personifies the knowledge that lies behind the creative process of life – or how and why things happen the way they do. For example, we say that like attracts like and that pride comes before a fall, and these phenomena are really the result of certain occult (hidden) laws.

When the High Priestess appears in a spread, we should be paying more careful attention to the psychic, intuitive world – it may have something to tell us.

**Key words for interpretation:** Hidden matters coming, however vaguely, to light; intuitive knowledge that can be applied to solving personal problems; wisdom; insight; may coincide with instructive dreams regarding future possibilities.

## 3 The Empress

A sensuous-looking woman holding an orb sits among the abundant manifestations of nature – ripe corn, verdant trees and a flowing stream. The red fruits depicted on her dress echo the symbol for Venus (infilled with the colour green), which itself appears inside a heart-shaped shield. On her head is a majestic crown of twelve stars.

This card bears the symbols of earthly bounty, fecundity and growth. If the High Priestess symbolises the mysteries of the spiritual world, the Empress embodies all that is material, natural and, indeed, part of the miracle of physical life. That the tallest tree began as a tiny seed, that with the return of summer the crops are newly ripe for harvesting, that our very bodies know how to heal and repair themselves ... these are all things we take for granted. But if you think about it, these natural growth patterns and regenerative cycles do have a sense of magic about them. Just think about the vastness and complexity of the information stored in the human DNA helix, for example.

The number three is essentially about creativity, for the synthesis of the one and the two equals a new product. If there is an underlying esoteric meaning for card number 3, it is that the manifestation of the physical world (and this can mean anything from flower blooms to the concrete events manifesting in our lives) always has some secret, organising intelligence. In other words, the material world is made up of a very complex relationship of hidden, though perfectly harmonised, factors, which modern physics calls – for want of a better term – energy. Occultists and mythographers, however, have always referred to this creative force in a more poetic way: the Great Mother. And so the synthesis and perfection of the three means that there is bountiful creation, material pleasure, growth and fruitfulness.

When the Empress appears in a key position in a spread, it is likely that you are experiencing (or will soon experience) a period of physical satisfaction at what life has to offer. There may be new creations, such as an artistic or business endeavour or the birth of a child. Whatever nature is providing at this time usually brings feelings of joy, physical comfort and security, and the promise of personal growth. In some packs the Empress is seated beside a massive cornucopia that spills its produce on to the earth.

When we get the Empress card in a reading, it is indeed time to benefit from the horn of plenty.

**Key words for interpretation:** The Great Mother principle in nature: nurture, growth, fertility (literal or metaphorical), abundance, domestic security, emotional comfort.

## 4 The Emperor

A mature, golden-crowned king sits on a carved, cubic throne holding an ankh and an orb. Four of the throne's corners are decorated with a ram's head. The colour of the background landscape is red (for spirit, action and passion), while the king's garments are an even deeper shade of red.

THE EMPEROR.

Here is the counterpart to the Empress, the archetypal father principle, without which life would be rendered chaotic and unworkable. If the Empress symbolises the fluidity and changeable quality of nature and its rhythms (and our ability to 'go with the flow'), the Emperor imposes himself upon the world in order to create stability, routine, order and a sense of authority. If the Empress is about being a part of nature, the Emperor, to an extent, stands outside nature in order to conquer and contain it. He thus represents that part of us that, in order to establish anything concrete in our lives, must achieve some measure of power, control and efficiency. This can only be done by an exercise of the will, by going out into the world to build up the resources necessary to establish our physical security, whatever challenges we may be confronted by.

The symbols of the active masculine principle (the colour red and the rams' heads, representative of the astrological Aries) are combined in this card with the 'four-ness' of physical stability and material form (the square throne, and the four rams' heads). These things together equate with dominion, worldly authority and the power of the creative will over the environment. Power and authority are also symbolised by the orb in the Emperor's left hand. As we have seen, the left is considered to be passive; in other words, the Emperor takes his power for granted.

When this card appears in a spread we are about to meet the archetypal father, and we may experience this in different ways. For male querents, it may mean literally becoming a father, or perhaps an encounter with the worldly and with material obligation in a broader sense. But the father archetype is not limited to men; all of us at some time will undergo a passage in life where we need to become our own authority, to stand on our own two feet and make something of ourselves. Of course, this also involves having to learn the lessons of responsibility (whether for ourselves or for others), for we cannot achieve, much less hold on to, worldly power (of whatever kind) without shouldering the weight of responsibility that comes with it.

**Key words for interpretation:** The father principle in nature; authority; power; responsibility; organisation; the means by which we gain concrete experience in the world; the conquering will applied to the concrete, material world.

## 5 The Hierophant

Between two ornate pillars, a red-robed Pope raises his right hand towards heaven; with his other hand he points a triple-crossed staff down to the earth. His golden crown has three tiers. Before him are two tonsured monks who receive his benediction. Between the monks is a pair of crossed keys.

If the High Priestess/Empress pair represents two different modes (spiritual and earthly, respectively) of the feminine principle, the Hierophant and the Emperor represent a similar masculine pair. Both are aspects of the same father principle, but one belongs to the earthly realm, while the other presides over the spiritual. However, the values of this spiritual father are certainly not limited to Christian doctrine; rather, he is the translator of all spiritual and philosophical knowledge available to the human world. If the High Priestess is protectress of occult knowledge (because much of it remains unconscious), then it is the purpose of the Hierophant, or high priest, to actively reveal the moral and philosophical laws that govern human nature and its relationship to God. The red in this card thus stands for action and expression, and the crossed keys symbolise spiritual revelation brought down to earth.

You do not need to be religious to appreciate that life is essentially meaningful, that there exists some mysterious creative source (whether within or without) that is greater than the individual. It is the purpose of philosophy to seek this meaningful source and describe the ways in which the inner world relates to the outer. The number three is about synthesis – the way in which two opposing entities are resolved by the addition of a third factor – and this card is full of motifs relating to the nature of three: the two kneeling figures form a triangular figure with the Hierophant in the centre; the crown has three tiers and the staff has three crosses; as does the Hierophant's vestment. The Hierophant, then, represents the synthesis and resolution of the eternal inner question: what is the meaning of life?

When this card appears in a spread we may be about to (or perhaps advised to) seek spiritual answers to the dilemma that is life, and perhaps to question how the disparate elements of our life might connect and come together as a meaningful whole. In a less philosophical sense, this may be a time to seek counsel and advice, or even healing of some kind. We may be ready to seek guidance from a teacher or other authority figure, or simply to reach out for inspiration and comfort.

**Key words for interpretation:** Spirituality and matters that draw us to the greater meaning of life; wholeness; teaching and enlightenment; healing; the seeking of wisdom and guidance from others.

## 6 The Lovers

The naked figures of Adam and Eve stand in the Garden of Eden. Behind Adam is the flaming Tree of Life; behind Eve is the Tree of the Knowledge of Good and Evil, with the serpent coiled about it. From out of a cloud appears a strange angelic being dressed in red and purple, who appears to preside over the pair below.

THE LOVERS.

Following on in numerical sequence from the spiritual and earthly aspects of the archetypal mother and father, we now have what might be called archetypal youth. Although this stage of development in life is symbolised by a pair of lovers, this card is about more than just the demands of love. The figures symbolise the universal pair of opposites, or all that is dual in both nature and the human psyche – good/evil, spiritual/earthly, active/ passive, passion/reason and so on.

On this card the male and female figures are ready to embark upon the journey towards true adulthood and all that entails, especially the experience of young love and burgeoning sexuality. It is natural that during this phase, we leave behind our parents in order to develop on a more individual path. This entails both difficulties and rewards, for when we leave behind a secure and stable phase of life we cannot be sure that the new one will offer similar support. In older packs, the image on this card depicted a young man choosing between his mother and his lover. The mother was a symbol of emotional security and the familiarity of the past, while the lover represented his true calling and life direction, together with the potential for true relationship through which he might discover himself.

The Adam and Eve myth of the Waite pack symbolises the desire for self-discovery and the eventual breakthrough of awareness when Eve tastes the forbidden fruit. Because Adam and Eve do not heed his warning, God banishes them from the Garden, and they come to know evil. But this new awareness of misfortune is a necessary prerequisite to becoming a fully rounded adult; through individual pain consciousness is gained. Our pain is not only educational but also engenders compassion for others.

When this card appears in a spread, a critical phase in our circumstances is implied. We may have to make a difficult choice (perhaps related to love) that is likely to set off a chain of events the outcome of which we cannot predict. This choice may also involve a moral issue, and we will have to call upon qualities of integrity, caution and maturity as we consider the best option. We are at a crossroads and in order to progress must decide which direction to take. Whatever decision we make, it will lead us further in the journey from youth to adulthood.

**Key words for interpretation:** The necessity of making a choice or decision; the need for maturity; a crossroads; possible difficult decisions within love, and the need to approach them in the most mature way.

## 7 The Chariot

A muscular charioteer stands in a stone chariot with a starry canopy. Before him are two sphinx-like figures. He is dressed in splendid clothes with lunar motifs. A laurel wreath and an eight-pointed crown encircle his head. He holds a wand loosely in his right hand.

The Chariot repeats the theme of duality and opposites that we encountered with the Lovers. With the Lovers, we had to make an important choice between two alternatives and were at loss as to how to make the choice. With the Chariot we have learned to rein in and contain this dichotomy; while the black and the white sphinxes still attempt to go in different directions, it is the will of the charioteer to master such opposites (anticipating the next card, Strength).

This card is concerned with power and mastery through self-willed action and independence – the kind that brings real success, for another divinatory meaning of this card is triumph. Note the charioteer's laurel wreath: he is victorious after a struggle. On an inner level, his victory is one of eventual awareness, which is to say that through confronting obstacles (whether inner or outer) he has obtained conscious wisdom. Awareness and knowledge won is symbolised by the card's yellow background.

But the idea of containment has subtler ramifications in this card, since traditionally the chariot itself represents the outer ego or persona. In other words, the mask we show to the world is a kind of protective outer vehicle within which we move through life; it protects the real self within. As we move out of childhood we learn to develop this external self, the public image, without doing violence to our inner emotional and instinctive side – our real self. Thus, ideally at least, we learn to keep things in balance as we proceed through life. Balance is represented in this card by the crescent moons at the charioteer's shoulders, which appear in perfect symmetry.

One of the keys to this card is the wand motif. Unlike the Magician's wand, it is not raised to heaven, calling upon external influences or help from above, but is rooted in physical strength, initiative and the successful force of will. However, the charioteer could not be successful through mere brute force – look at the triangular shape made by his body as it points towards the stars above his head and note the square at his breast. He has achieved a creative synthesis (triangle = three-ness) between what is within his grasp and the helping hand he may need from fate. And though success does not exactly fall into his lap, he is unconsciously guided towards making the right moves; his personal will is in harmony with the higher will, directed by an inner prescience and intuition that help to secure his progress through life.

When the Chariot appears in a spread, we often find ourselves, like the charioteer, in tune with our true destiny and intuitively taking steps to align with it.

**Key words for interpretation:** Triumph; success earned through application of the will; containment; inner strength; overcoming physical and psychological obstacles; progress.

## 8 Strength

A passive-looking woman, dressed in white and garlanded with roses, closes the jaws of a red lion. Above her head is a figure-of-eight halo, or lemniscate. The summit of a mountain can be seen in the distance, against a yellow background

A curious and subtle card, Strength is not about the suppression of base instincts, much less about repressing the ego. Repression suggests a conflict, whereas Strength is about a potential reconciliation of lower and higher selves (passions/emotions and intellect/reason) in which the rational mind brings firm resolve and steadfastness to the ever-shifting undercurrents of the feeling or instinctive world. The difference is that with Strength we are seeking to integrate such feelings, to acknowledge them and allow them to be. In the image on the card, this process is represented by the gentle pressure the woman exerts over the lion, as if taming it. Here, then, there is inner strength, the kind that comes from self-awareness and which generates a calm and firm resolve, as opposed to the extremes of being ruled by the passions or fearfully repressing them.

The presence of flower garlands and the lemniscate symbol (which also featured in the Magician card) is not accidental, for – like the Magician – on an esoteric level Strength represents the cyclic nature of the universe – what goes around comes around – and the philosophical truth that above and below are really a reflection of the same thing. Strength is, of course, also card number 8, and some writers have suggested that the flower garland on the woman's head connects to the flowers at her waist in such a way that it describes a figure eight around her. This is, then, a card about the potential for wholeness and for the reconciliation of mind and body in a creative way. The lower instincts symbolised by the lion (which can drive us into all sorts of self-defeating behaviour) are accepted as belonging to the entire self and are not wholly suppressed – just as the unruly behaviour of a child is reined in by a loving parent without quenching their spirit. This source of vitality is then seen for what it really is: survival instinct.

When this card appears in a spread it may indicate a struggle of some kind, for which we now require strength – the strength of gentle containment and standing fast with fortitude (Fortitude was an early name for this card) as the opposites rage within. This quality is often called grace under pressure and begets one the greatest gifts, understanding.

**Key words for interpretation:** Self-discipline in curbing certain impulses so that they do not gain the upper hand; steadfastness; resolve; inner reconciliation and integration; remaining calm and firm in the face of chaos and disruption.

## 9 The Hermit

A sombre-looking hermit dressed in a long hooded cowl looks down from his snow-capped mountain abode. He holds a long staff in his left hand, while in his right a lantern glows with a six-pointed star.

The solitary figure in the heights of the mountain obviously symbolises withdrawal, but we need to ask precisely why he has chosen this situation. Following on from the gentle fortitude of the preceding card, with which we learned to integrate 'higher' and 'lower', giving equal value to each, we are now removed entirely from the emotional realm and inhabit the rarefied atmosphere of the rational mind (represented by the mountain air). We are necessarily cut off from others here; we have put distance between ourselves and the human world in order to be free to think with clarity and precision. But such isolation and withdrawal does not only produce focus and clear-headed reason; it also activates our unconscious, intuitive side as we listen to that still, small voice within. Removal from the world of everyday human interaction thus leads to the journey within.

The Hermit depicts a man in old age, a familiar archetype in occult tradition, one that represents the slow passing of time and the wisdom of experience. The concept of the passage of time is linked to the virtue of patience, for it is through letting things take their natural course that we absorb certain life lessons. How many times have you heard it said that nothing worth having or doing was ever achieved in a hurry, whether this is a personal relationship, a career or a friendship? In short, such situations are better and richer for having matured slowly and gradually. Thus the Hermit is ultimately about the lessons of worldly wisdom – not the lightning intuitive flash of the brilliant quick-fire mind, but the patient, hard-earned wisdom of experience, symbolised by the light of the hermit's lantern.

When this card appears in a spread, the message is usually that we need to retire from external activities in order to gain a cool, calm and collected appreciation of our life situation – to slow down the pace and think issues over more carefully. We may need to realise our limitations, to accept that there is a need for patience and to understand that time changes everything.

**Key words for interpretation:** Withdrawal from the world; the need to take matters one at a time and perhaps seek advice; patience and an appreciation of the passage of time; learning from experience; limitations; looking at life dispassionately, coolly and rationally.

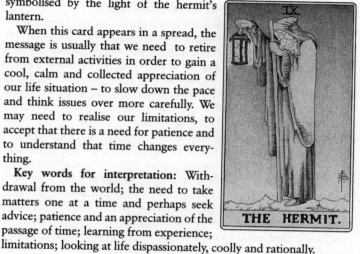

THE HERMIT.

## 10 The Wheel of Fortune

An eight-spoked wheel hangs in the upper realms; astride the wheel is a sphinx holding a sword. Ascending on the left-hand side of the wheel is a curious, jackal-headed figure; descending on the right-hand side is a serpent. Around the circumference of the wheel are the letters TARO.

WHEEL of FORTUNE.

In the four corners of the image are symbols representing the four fixed signs of astrology: Taurus, Leo, Scorpio and Aquarius.

It is no surprise that the sphinx, associated with the cycle of life and death, should sit on top of the wheel, presiding over the mystery that is fate, destiny or karma. The motif of the wheel makes plain that everything in our existence is subject to cyclical change. We need only think of the cycle of the seasons to grasp this idea of circularity; what may not be quite so obvious is that our entire lives are made up of cycles within cycles. The physical cycle (our birth, growth, ageing and death) itself encompasses emotional and intellectual cycles of developing awareness. And, of course, other aspects of our existence go in cycles.

Whatever the various aspects of our lives have become – for example in our career or personal relationships – they must be kept in good shape in order to remain meaningful and rewarding in some way. Without life in them, they will wither and die. Often, however, when something has truly run its course, it will die no matter how we want to hold on to it. The experience no longer fulfils us because we are no longer the same with respect to the outer situation. This is particularly so in relationships. How often do we hear about partners drifting apart despite their best efforts to keep things together? Although the inner changes they have undergone may be involuntary, they have essentially grown and moved on in some way.

At the root of all such cycles is what we might call fate, but this is not mere blind chance – quite the reverse. It can also be seen as an orderly pattern whereby inner transformation finally brings about outer changes, though the inner significance can often be detected only after the outer event has occurred – we can see the path we are on only one step at a time.

When this card appears in a spread, a major step in our destiny is usually indicated. A significant change of circumstance, either sudden or gradual, may be in the offing. The Wheel is bound up with the processes of time: how we effect changes in our lives and how life, in turn, changes us. Like the serpent on the left-hand side of this card, we may be taking a downturn in our fortunes; conversely, we may be about to move upwards on the other side towards a new success as the ever rotating wheel of life keeps on turning.

**Key words for interpretation:** Change that is often irrevocable and seemingly fated; a brand new cycle of events – whether good or bad will be suggested by other surrounding cards; karma and the reaping of what has been sown in past actions.

## 11 Justice

An impassive-looking woman sits on a throne between two stone pillars; in her right hand she holds an upright sword, in her left a pair of scales. She is dressed in red robes and wears a golden crown. The square motif appears on her crown and as a clasp that holds a cloak around her neck.

We have already seen a female figure seated between two pillars: the High Priestess, presiding over the mystery of life's duality and archetypal opposites. In Justice, the woman sits sternly between two stark, granite pillars. Here, there is only cold detachment and little real mystery at all. The red and green colours worn by Justice symbolise direct action and earthly productivity: the judgements reached by this archetype are meant to engender practical results in the physical world. The justice at stake here is that to do with human beings and the laws that they create and enact, as opposed to the karmic judgement of the Wheel or the cosmic judgement we will later meet in Trump 20 (Judgement).

The squares (earth) that Justice wears show that her judgements have a real function in the concrete world, and it is we who are being judged. That is to say, the Justice card is about matters of morality. All of us instinctively know (even in a modern age where moral absolutes seem to change every year) what is right and what is wrong. The unconscious seems to contain an in-built sense of conscience; guilt at having done wrong does not seem to be a learned response. Hence, the figure of Justice exists somewhere within us – we are our own judges.

When Justice appears in a significant position in a spread, we are about to be weighed in the balance. The Justice figure holds a pair of finely balanced scales. Look more closely at the gesture she makes: the sword in her right hand (decisions we have made, actions we have taken) points upwards, while the scales in her left hand, along with her index finger, point down to earth. Thus our actions are about to bear some kind of physical fruit in the here and now. We are about to receive our just desserts – nothing more or nothing less than we deserve. This is simply because the forces we have set in motion need to be balanced out in some way. It is really no more than Isaac Newton's law of action and reaction: every force acting upon the universe (i.e. our thoughts and actions) has an equal and opposite reaction.

When this card appears in a spread, it is time to take full responsibility for what we have done. There is no other way to go about this than to remain quietly detached and reasonable, and to see the situation from a balanced perspective.

**Key words for interpretation:** Individual conscience, morality and objective truth; the need for an impartial, fair and wholly rational view of things; the law, arbitration and settling disputes.

## 12 The Hanged Man

This is one of the Tarot's most striking images: a young man with a glowing halo around his head is inverted on a T-shaped cross. His crossed left leg depicts a figure four in reverse and his arms are behind his torso. He wears red tights and a pale blue tunic.

As has often been noted by other writers, the passive expression on the face of the Hanged Man suggests that his suspension from the cross is a voluntary one. The red tights (representing the active, solar principle) and the figure four (standing for earthly matters) are prominent, yet they have been turned upside-down, thus symbolising

the inversion of the ego, worldly values and the way in which we usually operate in life. The kind of awareness open to us here is therefore one of seeing the whole picture – looking at life not through fragmentary and prejudiced opinions but as it really is. With the Hanged Man we approach matters with a more gentle and intuitive feel for the situation, letting life happen to us, as opposed to holding it at a distance with cold logic and rational analysis.

But how many of us are prepared to give up our habitual ways of perceiving, much less of living our lives without our precious identities? How many of us can be bothered even to entertain the idea that we may be something more than our limited egos? This is the esoteric meaning of the Hanged Man – that something of greater value lies within, something that requires effort, patience and courage to discover. The Hanged Man is suspended between the limited perceptions of the physical world (those engendered by the senses) and the forceful depths of the unconscious. He is at a midpoint where he can see that there is more to the material world than meets the eye, and yet he is safe from being drowned in the sea of unconsciousness (dream states and overwhelming emotions) that would prevent him from making rational sense of his perceptions. This 'living in suspension' is the key to interpreting this card and relates to a transition period in our life, specifically one where we have willingly given something up (or will have to do so) to obtain something else of greater value.

Thus we arrive at this card's esoteric meaning, that of willing sacrifice – because of a faith that, in making this sacrifice, we will eventually be vindicated. There is a magical precedent for this kind of sacrifice, that of the law of the distribution of energy. If you want to attract the good things of life by using magic, you must be prepared to carry out all the necessary mental and emotional work that will make your goal happen. If you are successful, what has happened is nothing more than one form of expended energy (your rituals) coming back as another (your physical results). All of which sounds wonderful, but the kind of sacrifices necessary on the magical path (in terms of mental discipline) are daunting enough to discourage most people. That is why genuine sacrifices – where we give up something we truly value – often lead to unexpected rewards.

When you get this card in a reading, it is likely that you are at a crossroads and have important decisions to make. You may not realise the benefits of your decisions immediately, but you will gain advantages in one way or another from doing the right thing.

**Key words for interpretation:** Voluntary sacrifice so that something greater can come along; life in suspension; adapting to outer circumstances; getting a sense of life's flow and rhythm; letting go and trusting life; inner guidance from the intuitive part of the mind.

## 13 Death

The first thing to stress here is that this card must not be taken literally. A skeletal figure in black armour, holding a banner depicting a white rose, rides his white horse heedlessly through a field of motley human figures: a dead king, a child, a maiden and bishop. Behind the bishop, the sun sinks on the horizon between a two-pillared gateway. Beyond the gate, a distant city is silhouetted before the sun.

This card is far less ambiguous than the preceding one. Death is a fact of life, and kings, bishops and children alike must eventually face it. It is of significance that in this image only the child looks upon death – while the bishop prays and the maiden turns away. Only true innocence, or a free spirit, can have the courage to countenance death, which is to say that the more worldly we become, the more we cling to life and the more we fear death.

There is much alchemical symbolism in the Death card. Esoterically, it often indicates the end of a current phase or situation. This entails letting go of the old (and as soon as possible, too) so that the new can be born. This death may also be a stage in a psychological process – the death, if you will, of a part of ourselves. The psyche is always seeking growth and awareness in order to become more conscious of itself and the world. Inevitably, the time comes when we have done with a certain inner phase in our lives, with its attendant emotional habits, attitudes and values. As the newer self emerges and we begin to care about different things, an old self must die. The process can be likened to the shedding of an old skin, revealing a new one underneath. This shedding often occurs in the aftermath of a personal crisis, but not always. Sometimes, it is just part of a natural process of psychological development. Nor can we stop it. We change – or rather we grow –

whether we like or not, and such change always involves a death of some kind.

Of course, phases of personal transition are rarely easy, often involving a good deal of pain. In alchemy this is symbolised by the *nigredo*, or blackening phase, when our spirit descends to the depths of the unconscious and dissolves before it can be purified and finally renewed. Look closely at the bishop's mitre on the Death card; it looks (not unintentionally) like the jaws of a crocodile, which appear to be swallowing the sun. The image of the lower devouring the higher is a traditional Hermetic motif; sometimes a wolf eats a dead king. It means simply that when the time comes we must relinquish our precious ego, our self-image, and even our noblest and most spiritual aspirations, and give way to this natural process of death and eventual rebirth. We must simply let it happen, no matter how much it hurts, if anything is to change for the better.

If you get this card in a reading it is important to be aware that it does not relate to an actual death; rather it indicates a time of natural change, of one phase ending and another beginning. It may not be easy to move ahead – there may be some sadness in leaving aspects of your life behind – but there will be new challenges ahead.

**Key words for interpretation:** The need to accept the end of a situation; clinging to the past; renewal, regeneration and transformation; clearing the decks for a new phase in life (which can only occur when we have relinquished the old one); outer forms that die and change while the inner essence or spirit remains.

## 14 Temperance

A winged angel in white raiment pours liquid from one vessel, in her left hand, to another, in her right. On her brow is a solar disk, at her breast a triangle motif. She stands with one foot immersed in the pool before her.

The previous two cards both include an emblem of the spirit whose light is about to wane (the glowing halo of the Hanged Man and the setting sun of Death). Fading daylight symbolises a turning away from the outer conscious life and towards inner concerns; dusk is a time for reflection and the sifting of emotional impressions. Likewise, in Temperance, the sun sets in the distance behind the angel; we are still in the realm of the unconscious, still subject to its outworkings and must co-operate by maintaining a sense of harmony in our life, moving too far in neither direction. That is, we must find a balance between the opposite forces of intellect and emotion. The angel of Temperance has one foot in the watery depths and the other on dry land; in other words, she stands between the selfishness of raging ego desires and the calm, patient acknowledgement that there is a whole world out there to which we must adapt.

When this card appears, the issue of needing to reconcile certain opposites is usually present, and we must somehow try to steer the middle path, to find the happy medium. The ego dissolution of Death has rendered the psyche a collection of contradictions and opposites – light and shadow, good and evil. The angel of Temperance appears here as a kind of bridging force, counselling moderation in all things.

If the old forms or situations are now a thing of the past, the life force and spirit are certainly not. They are symbolised here by the triangle, its apex pointing upwards, within the square, and the solar disk that glows at the angel's head. If we are in pain as a result of what Death has removed from our lives, Temperance moves us towards equilibrium, healing and internal balance – as long as we have patience, for such matters cannot be hurried. The water she pours from one vessel to another depicts nature's flow (and hence the psyche's) – its tendency to self-regulate and balance itself out, moving from light to dark and back to light again, yet never exclusively one or the other all of the time.

When this card appears in a spread, we need to go with the flow, as it were, avoiding all extremes as we mediate our way through life.

**Key words for interpretation:** Reconciliation of opposites; the need for moderation, self-control and appropriate behaviour; the development of a sense of proportion in all things, whether a balanced heart or a dispassionate attitude to life.

## 15 The Devil

A horned figure with huge bat's wings and an inverted pentagram at its forehead presides over the gloom of Hades. His torso is human, his legs those of a goat. In his left hand he holds a torch that points downwards and with his right hand he gestures up. A young man and woman – the Lovers of card number 6 – are chained to the rectangular dais on which he sits. Wearing horns, they are debased, the sun and the angelic figure of the Lovers card having become Satan and the night.

The Lovers (card 6) and the Devil (card 15) are linked by the magical number nine (15 – 6 = 9). If we reduce the number 15 to its root (by adding both digits together), we arrive at six (1 + 5 = 6). The connection between cards 6 and 9 is indicated by the coiled serpent of the former, which in the latter simply assumes its more recognisable form as the Devil.

This is one of the more controversial images in the Major Arcana. Its Judaeo-Christian connections are unavoidable, though many writers have pointed out that the figure is the pre-Christian Pan of Greek mythology, the phallic (horned) personification of the instinctive, regenerative forces in nature. The inverted five-pointed star (man) and upturned flaming wand show that spirit has (as in trumps 12, 13 and 14) been turned upside-down.

The Devil is, in some ways, the reverse of Temperance. The upright triangle is here turned upside-down to become the head of the Devil, his beard tapering off to a point. The angel of Temperance stands in the cool light of day, a symbol of balance, whereas the Devil appears against stark blackness, a symbol of extremes. Here, the spirit, the *summum bonum*, or highest good, is itself degraded; all that is of value here is appetite, base instincts and the demands of the body.

As in Temperance, here the theme of opposites looms large: the ego and the shadow; the conscious self and the darker, unintegrated contents of the psyche. No matter how civilised we think we are with our spiritual ideals and intellect, we are still in truth half animal, with base urges that refuse to be ignored, be they appetite for food, sex or aggression. This animal behaviour surfaces all the time, and we repress it at our peril, for we attract what we deny. If the Devil card warns us of anything, it is that to submerge the instincts constantly beneath a patina of so-called civilised behaviour is just as bad as becoming enslaved to them.

However, throwing off the shackles of dark, emotional drives and the demands of the body is, with a little self-discipline, not that difficult. Note the nooses on the chains that restrain the Adam and Eve figures – they are large enough to allow them to escape if they really want to. The two figures have actually embraced this narrow and materialistic state of affairs – they are there of their own accord.

When this card appears in a spread, we may need to stand back and consider whether we too are willingly enslaving ourselves to our physical or emotional urges. We are also free to leave whenever we like; all we need to do is confront our own darkness by accepting it.

**Key words for interpretation:** Enslavement or obsession to an idea, an emotion or the physical senses; the need to face and integrate our darker side; over-attachment to the material world and symbols of security.

81

## 16 The Tower

A lightning-blasted stone tower bursts into flames in the dead of night. Its occupants, a king and queen, are thrown violently from the building, while a huge crown is likewise toppled. The colours turquoise and red are prominent on the king and queen.

The sequence from card 15, the Devil, to card 16, the Tower, is easy to see: our attachment to the physical universe, to our possessions and to our status is ripped apart through a crisis. But why such a fearful image? We all become accustomed to a certain degree of regularity and security in our lives; indeed, we could not live without this. However, there sometimes comes a point where what once gave comfort and support becomes dull routine – and eventually stifling and suffocating. The more tightly we hold on to life, the more resistant we are to change; and the more we insist that whatever we have constructed remains permanent, the more insecure and vulnerable it becomes.

To be truly creative and meaningful, life must change, and we must go with it. The energies inherent in the universe must be allowed to flow. If we attempt to erect permanent structures that take no account of this river of life force, the universal energies are likely to come crashing through. This is not mere misfortune that happens to us, but rather the result of a situation we have created. Raw life-force will attempt to break through when it can no longer exist within these confines.

This is really what is occurring in the image on the Tower. The massive crown falling from on high is the overturned ego. Our former world becomes inverted and what we have complacently become used to no longer exists in the same way. The old forms are breaking down – not so much due to a process of nature, as in Death, as to human ignorance. The red and blue of the royal couple's clothing symbolise both willpower and emotions, which are here cast aside as useless and irrelevant. The will can do nothing to change the situation; what has been destroyed is gone for good. Nor does the universe care about our personal feelings; there is little in the way of reassurance and comfort.

But there is another way of seeing this situation – one that will rarely be apparent at the time of such a crisis. The lightning bolt, despite the havoc it creates, can renew and revivify our life if we allow it to. If we do not cling too tightly, that overriding sense of insecurity in the aftermath of emotional loss can be quite heady – even exciting – as we face the future, for now something new can happen. We may have lost what we had, but now there is the possibility of gaining something entirely new. This card represents what is truly the lowest ebb in the Major Arcana, but from now on things can only improve.

When this card appears in a spread, it indicates that areas of doubt are clearing and new options are opening up. It may be that something that appeared to be a setback has, in fact, allowed an area of our life to be rebuilt in a positive way. It could also indicate that we would like to make a change to something that may be holding us back.

**Key words for interpretation:** The breaking down of old forms; destruction; the need for a clean sweep where something is based on false values or inadequate support; self-delusion leading to self-undoing.

## 17 The Star

A naked young woman kneels before a pool. Above her head is an eight-pointed star; seven smaller stars make a total of eight in all. The woman holds a water-filled pitcher in each hand; from the pitcher in her left hand she pours water into the pool, while with the pitcher in her right hand she replenishes the land.

After the devastation of the Tower, here there is the promise of renewal – the sense that there is light at the end of the tunnel. In the Greek myth, Pandora foolishly opens a box containing everything that might afflict the human race – infirmity, madness, old age, drudgery, vice. All these calamities rapidly fly out and go about their business, visiting misery and evil upon men and women. Pandora hastens to shut the lid of the box, but all that is left there is hope. This story is a metaphor for what happens when utter misfortune has visited us – only hope remains. If we can at least find a little hope in our hearts, then all is not lost.

The nakedness of the woman in the Star is symbolic of the removal of whatever is unnecessary to the individual's life – the trappings of the outer self – in order that the renewal process can begin. In other words, it is time to focus on what really matters, on what is natural and on the fundamental needs of the spirit. (You will notice that the final three trumps of the Major Arcana all depict naked figures.)

From the shattered illusions and material destruction of the Tower to the willing embrace of truth and simplicity in the Star, the progression is quite easy to see. If we consider the water in the pool as going into the pitcher that the woman holds in her right hand and coming out of the pitcher in her left hand and on to the land, then she is herself a kind of vessel. She is, like Temperance, a mediator of the flow of life itself, an archetype that shows us how the raw stuff of the unconscious (the pool) with its mysterious creative power can be used for our benefit, replenishing mind and body. With both her right limbs connecting with the pool, the woman is actively engaged in seeking out the depths, quietly but determinedly turning inwards for insight and guidance. Her kneeling posture – a traditional sign of obeisance – is a gesture of obedience to something more powerful. Here, the power lies in the inner forces that offer healing and point the way towards new life.

When this card appears in a spread, we may be about to acquire new hope, even faith, that will help in a current predicament. Even if our life is not presently difficult, new insights appropriate to current plans or possibilities that lie ahead may still be made available. Whatever our situation in life, the Star of hope lights our way.

**Key words for interpretation:** Hope; the promise of renewal; the need for faith; gentle insights that help us to see ahead and accept the past; healing; rebirth.

## 18 The Moon

A large crayfish emerges from a pool on to dry land, where a dog and a wolf bark at the moon. The lunar orb pictured here is superimposed over the sun, creating an eclipse, beneath which dew drops fall between the two stone towers that featured in Death.

THE MOON.

The lunar face that looks down in solemn repose here is that of the Greek moon goddess Artemis. (In earlier Tarot packs, this face is explicitly female.) In Greek myth each of the three lunar phases is associated with a particular goddess; the waxing moon is the maiden Persephone; the full moon is the mature woman Demeter; and the waning moon is the old woman Hecate (who appears as Queen of the Night and possessor of magical powers in the Marseilles Tarot). These figures represent the archetypal feminine, symbolising all that is dark, mysterious, irrational and unconscious – and consequently, powerful, awe-inspiring and fearful to those of a more rational turn of mind. They represent not only the inner depths on an individual level but also the collective unconscious. They are the universal womb from which all life springs, but also the tomb in which all life ends.

If we have glimpsed hope and a sense of incipient change in the Star card, here we must trust in a way forward that seems to have little light at all. All here is uncertain, unsure and tentative. Our future may appear vague and cloudy when this card turns up in a spread. The pool that appeared in the Star is now seen to contain a primal creature, the crayfish. Likewise, the red dog and the white wolf stand for the forces of irrationality, that which devours our sense of ourselves as clear-thinking and purposeful human beings with a firm sense of identity. They are madness itself – the loss of the ego-self, consciousness usurped by the unconscious and all its shadowy denizens.

During this uncertain phase we must overcome our fear of these realms; we must trust that we will make it through the night-time of confusion and dream-like uncertainty. With its turquoise-blue colours (representing the watery realm of the emotions) the Moon card depicts a passage through life that is under the spell of the lunar, feminine forces. When we make this passage, we offer up our conscious self just as we do to sleep each night.

When this card appears in a spread, willpower, logic and meticulous planning are probably useless. We may be confused about what our next move should be and in the dark regarding the outcome of certain projects. Even if we are moving confidently through life, we need to guard against over-optimism – we never really know when the forces of delusion are at work.

**Key words for interpretation:** A period of indecision, doubt and uncertainty; the need for patience, courage and faith in the future; the need to avoid seductive illusions; a time to rely on intuition for guidance.

## 19 The Sun

Inside a walled garden containing sunflowers, a joyous infant figure with a red feather in his hair rides on the back of a white horse, raising a huge red banner to the sky. Above, the sun shines in magnificent splendour.

After the uncertain, illusion-strewn path of the Moon, daylight has finally dawned. On a superficial level the image of the Sun is straightforward to interpret: a new joy and sense of optimism about life; however, the process that has led to this archetypal stage of development is often far more complex. In fact, its nature depends on precisely what course our life has taken. Much of the imagery of this card derives from alchemy. The triumphal red banners, the sunflowers and the celebratory child are related to the Red King of Hermetic thought. This child is sometimes depicted in alchemy as a homunculus, the new, pure and innocent product of an experiment, born in an alchemical retort. The infant we see here thus symbolises a renewed and deepened faith in life following a painful situation.

Life can sometimes seem confusing and uncertain; there may be periods of emotional loss and depression when we cannot see ahead clearly and seem to have no purchase on our future. Often we are still in thrall to the past, still tainted by our former situation. Only through the passage of time, which enables a kind of inner healing to take place, does clarity arise, with the promise of a new future and the sense that we are somehow reborn. We have, as it were, died to the past, and the child within us is full of joy and optimism.

Alchemically, this card relates to the stage of approaching perfection; we have undergone the purification stage, the 'whitening', and the dross has been burned away. The *rubedo,* or reddening, is now about to take place. This is symbolised by the red banner held by the child, which promises vitality and a passion for living.

When this card appears in a spread, there is every reason to feel optimism about the future, whatever we have planned. The walled garden in which the jubilant infant finds himself is a protective Eden where he can remain safe in his new sense of trust. Having passed through the darkness and trial of faith required by the Moon, we are here vindicated, but we have changed in the process. We have the youthful vigour to see the old situation with new eyes, through the light of clarity and simplicity, untainted by cynicism or gloom.

**Key words for interpretation:** Success; joy; pleasure; optimism; a new faith in life; the development of confidence and self-belief, and its vindication in the outer world.

## 20 Judgement

An archangel with red wings sounds a trumpet at the Last Judgement. To the trumpet is attached a banner with a red cross on a white background. The dead rise from their graves out of the sea, while in the foreground is a trio of newly resurrected figures: a man, a woman and a child, all naked.

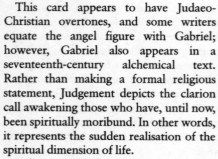

This card appears to have Judaeo-Christian overtones, and some writers equate the angel figure with Gabriel; however, Gabriel also appears in a seventeenth-century alchemical text. Rather than making a formal religious statement, Judgement depicts the clarion call awakening those who have, until now, been spiritually moribund. In other words, it represents the sudden realisation of the spiritual dimension of life.

Judgement develops some of the ideas present in the previous card, the Sun. In fact, the final three cards of the Major Arcana form a kind of triptych, whose meanings interrelate. The red of the banner borne aloft by the child in the Sun now appears in the angel's wings and in the cross symbol on the banner attached to the trumpet. Crosses, you will remember, are about 'four-ness', solidity and integration; in this card the cross represents matters coming to a head. The coffins from which the figures arise as they float on the sea are womb-like containers (rather like the walled garden of the Sun) that have thus far protected the growing embryos now ready to appear in the world. We are probably all familiar with the psychological process whereby at certain periods of major transition in our lives something new – some new sense of profound awareness or new emotional or psychological reality – is born within us.

In the external world, this energy may manifest as an idea whose time has finally come. The time may be ripe to develop a new project, a previously uncertain matter may become clear, or we may at last be put in the picture. This is not quite a reward for past efforts, although in a spread Judgement can indeed signify karmic just desserts. It is more that we are now in a much better position to understand the meaning of what is happening in our lives. This may be a time for looking back at the past to see our mistakes and gain some understanding from them.

When you get this card in a reading, it is time to listen to the call of the archangel's trumpet blast and perhaps to embrace a different attitude to some facet of our life or being. A new awareness is made available, one appropriate to our newly reborn self.

**Key words for interpretation:** A time of things coming to light, when we can finally act perhaps after a period of being in the dark; a situation that has crystallised and changed in some way; karmic results; the consequences of our actions made clear, possibly giving rise to a new phase in life.

## 21 The World

Against a rich blue background (like that of the previous two cards) is the figure of *anima mundi* (the soul of the world), who dances naked but for the purple sash that entwines her. She holds a wand in each hand. Around her is an elliptical wreath held together with red material. The figures symbolising the four elements, or fixed zodiac signs, appear one in each corner of the image.

There is really no way to represent fully the mystery that is life in total – the force that really makes things happen, that is behind why we are here, where we came from and where we are going. However, the *anima mundi* is one of the most complete symbols of totality and wholeness, of union and reconciliation of opposites. The four elements necessary to life (and to our inner sense of wholeness) are represented here by the bull (Earth), the lion (Fire), the eagle (Water) and the human (Air), which together form a complete system. The greenery that wreaths the dancer is shaped like the figure 0 (infinite potential), or like an egg (out of which new life hatches). It is also reminiscent of the ouroboros, the serpent in the act of eating its own tail, a representation of infinity and of the way in which life perpetually renews itself.

The World is the only card in the Major Arcana from which duality, opposites and their implied tension is missing. Everything resolves into the one and perfect symmetry is achieved as our eyes are drawn to the figure in the centre. The dancer is neither exclusively male nor exclusively female but a hermaphrodite. (The purple sash hides the figure's genitals.) Thus male and female, active and passive, light and dark, positive and negative are reconciled and integrated within the one being. The figure dances because she/he is a part of the rhythmic flow of life itself. To live life successfully and completely at all levels of our being, we must embrace change, go with the flow, partake in the dance of life. Thus we become one with life, and there is no ultimate difference between the dancer and the dance, the doer and the deed, the thinker and the thought. We are simply caught up in living life in the moment.

Like the naked adult and child figures in the Sun and Judgement cards, the dancing figure here is also a new-born creation, a symbolic conjunction of both male and female reconciled. In Hermetic thought, this is the successful manufacture of the philosopher's stone, alchemical gold – the spiritual treasure that after a long struggle we have finally discovered in ourselves. It represents the triumph of light over darkness, awareness over ignorance.

When this card appears in a spread, something has finally – or is about to – come together, for this is a card of fulfilment and successful manifestation, on either an inner or an outer level

**Key words for interpretation:** The successful completion of a certain matter; the attainment of goals or the culmination of a particular cycle of events; fulfilment and synthesis; wholeness and a sense of satisfaction; reward for previous efforts.

# Chapter 5
# The Minor Arcana –
# the Suit of Wands

We have already looked in outline at the Minor Arcana, with its four suits of Wands, Cups, Swords and Pentacles, with Ace to Ten plus Page, Knight, Queen and King in each suit. The next four chapters will look in more detail at each of the cards in turn, starting in this chapter with the Wands.

Wands are associated with Fire, inspiration and achievement, as well as the destruction of anything that is no longer necessary.

## Ace of Wands

Out of a cloud appears a huge wooden staff, or wand, held firmly by a mysterious right hand. The wand illuminates a dusky landscape below.

Here is the basic life energy, the spirit, that which makes us want to live life at all. This life-giving force is symbolised by Fire, in the Tarot

represented by the suit of Wands, that magical tool that calls upon the primal and potent forces of the universe to effect any magical spell. In a spread, the Ace (new energies) of Wands thus stands for an upsurge of creative power, the readiness to embark upon a new enterprise, and the new ideas associated with any endeavour. There tends now to be an emphasis on the new and untried, a sense that perhaps anything is possible, and, as such, this card has neutral connotations – we cannot tell just yet what the outcome will be. But we are more than ready, and full of optimism for the success of whatever is about to commence.

**Key sentence for interpretation:** There is readiness and a great deal of energy to take new initiatives.

## Two of Wands

A pensive red-robed man looks out from a high wall on to a calm bay. He stands between two staves, one of which is held in his left hand. In his right hand there is a small globe. To the left of him is a cross formation of red roses and white lilies.

This card is traditionally linked with the theme of dominion. The figure in the picture is usually taken to represent the conqueror of territory who now rests awhile, overseeing his domain yet seeming to derive no great pleasure from his accomplishments. The card has a double edge, for the principle of 'two-ness' (duality, division) combined with the Fire principle means that energy might easily be wasted in needless distractions. When this card appears in a spread, there is much unfulfilled potential that must, nevertheless, be harnessed and directed by the will into worthwhile endeavours. We met the white (potential) lilies and red (action) roses in the Magician card; similarly, the Two of Wands is about the requirement for controlled action, about getting the most from ourselves by truly special effort and the pursuit of excellence, for only that way do we achieve any authority over life.

**Key sentence for interpretation:** We need to call upon strength to make genuine progress and realise our goals.

## *Three of Wands*

We see the back of a male figure looking out to sea; there are three staves behind him, one of which he gently holds. There are low hills in the distance.

A less ambiguous card than the Two, the Three of Wands similarly

depicts a calm figure gazing out over a landscape, but note how the staff is this time in the man's right hand, right being the direction connected with the positive, active principle. This man is seen amidst the natural landscape, whereas the Two figure required the security of his walled domain. Hence he is far more content with his achievements so far, and is free on a deeper level because, not needing to be walled in, he is ready to adapt to any and every external circumstance. Like the sailing ships below him, he is prepared to explore new territories. This is the kind of success created not by strenuous effort but by ease and confidence. The energy here is flowing positively and creatively (as we

might expect from 'three-ness'). This card denotes early success in a particular venture, and the feelings of confidence and strength that accompany such a reward.

**Key sentence for interpretation:** There will be initial successes, a sense of power and inspiration, and the possibility of turning ideas into reality.

## _Four of Wands_

In the foreground, four tall staves are garlanded with roses; in the background, two happy figures lift flower bouquets aloft outside a walled city.

The confident expectation of the Three has led to barely contained joy here in the Four. There is a sense of satisfaction, happiness and, most importantly, security. The Four seems to complete a cycle of events that sprang to life in the Ace, from initial energy to successfully finished product. There is a sense of inner stability, with the city walls representing security – that special something to fall back on. We have capitalised on the early success of the Three and now have occasion to celebrate contentment with our present environment. The two happy central figures in this card are midway between the city (material existence) behind them, and the four staves (spirit) in front. Thus they represent integration and wholeness, the outer life in harmony with the inner. This is therefore a card of stability and completion.

**Key sentence for interpretation:** We enjoy security and happiness due to positive achievements.

## Five of Wands

Five young men armed with staves and dressed in an array of colours seem to be staging a mock battle. The whole scene is one of disarray. There is the makings of a crude triangle (harmony) , but this is pierced through by another stave.

The stability of the Four gives way to a new struggle, but these are often tests of patience that cannot be avoided. In short, the kinds of conflict represented by the Five of Wands are those closely bound up with the fabric of our very existence. Just as the young men in the image are really only playing rather than seriously fighting, the irritations that come with the Five are often only of the minor kind and just have to be put up with. Only great ingenuity and forethought can prevent them. Think of Murphy's Law: 'If something can go wrong, it probably will'. The frustration encountered here is really self-inflicted, for these problems are largely insoluble and just have to be tolerated. We must simply adapt to the necessities of the slow-moving, concrete world.

**Key sentence for interpretation:** We may have to pay attention to the limits of the material world and could have our patience tested.

## Six of Wands

This card has obvious suggestions of victory won. The rider in the foreground wears a laurel wreath on his head and holds up a large staff, also crowned with laurel. He is followed by other riders.

The apparent victory parade depicted on this card is in fact rather ambiguous. Is this really a public display in the wake of a military triumph, or are the riders on their way into battle? The crowning wreaths suggest the former, and yet there is very little truly martial about this image. Most of the traditional interpretations focus upon the idea of victory after strife, of having won out over the frustrations and setbacks of the Five, but this card also can signify that our achievement is recognised in some special way by others. It stands for victory occasioned by the faith we have had in life – life has vindicated us and others now acknowledge it. In other instances, this card can signify acclaim and support from those in power, hence some kind of public reward such as a job promotion or general recognition of our talents.

**Key sentence for interpretation:** There is a sense of winning out, victory and achievement, together with acknowledgement and encouragement from others.

## Seven of Wands

A young warrior positioned on the edge of a precipice anxiously defends himself against unseen assailants, who between them wield against him six staves.

This is an image of courage and bravery in which the individual takes

on others simultaneously. All the emboldened forces of will are present. The man in the picture is ready to take on whatever life throws at him. However, there are various ways of interpreting this card. The pitting of ourselves against some form of opposition may refer to an internal battle in which we are divided against ourselves over some current life matter. It may be an issue where we are required to have the courage of our convictions and go ahead with a vital decision we feel to be right. Or this may be a more literal kind of struggle, against some individual or group. In either case, however, we are called upon to summon inner strength and outdo some formidable competition. The strong implication is that this is now the only proper way forward. To back down would be fatal.

**Key sentence for interpretation:** We are facing powerful opposition, and adversaries may be as strong as we are.

## Eight of Wands

Eight staves fly swiftly through the air. Below them, in contrast, is an image of calm: low hills and a still lake.

If in the Seven we had to do battle, here we are able to move swiftly ahead, unimpeded by any opposition. In fact, swiftness is one of the keywords traditionally associated with this card, and it quite often indicates swift progress following recent setbacks with which we have had to deal. The more occult meaning of this card lies in the fact that all the Wands in the image are parallel and are finally descending to earth (they are not at the beginning of their trajectory). The Eight of Wands therefore augurs well; our creative ideas and plans are well thought out and are about to materialise. At the very least, this card suggests a speedy resolution of any problems and a sense of movement and progress.

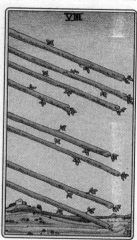

**Key sentence for interpretation:** There will be swiftness and progress in plans, together with an end to delays and upheavals.

## Nine of Wands

A rather beleaguered young man, his head bandaged after a recent injury, stands at rest, holding a large staff. Eight more staves form a defensive wall behind him.

This image is fairly straightforward. It represents that sense of being

up against it but nevertheless not willing to give in just yet. The man's angry expression and his readiness with the large staff he holds show that he is ready to fight another day if necessary. There is a kind of strength in the defensive position we are adopting when this card appears in a spread, but there is a warning too – about tilting at windmills. Not every competitive situation we encounter is a potential threat! Study the image more carefully. The centrally positioned stave divides the picture into left and right. On the right-hand side, the defensive wall has been breached by the man's removal of one of the staves, to which he now clings for protection. This is ironical: the more tightly we hug the symbols of security, the less secure we feel. In other words, our sheer defensiveness can prove a drawback: it prevents us from going ahead with confidence. The natural exuberance and strength of the Wands is in danger of exhausting itself, of turning into its own opposite.

**Key sentence for interpretation:** Although we are able to find strength in adversity, we may be too much on the defensive.

## Ten of Wands

A heavily laden figure carries ten large staves to a nearby town.

On one level it is obvious what this image represents: the danger of taking on too many responsibilities and obligations, for these are likely to weigh us down before too long. The traditional keyword for this card is oppression. How we got here, according to the progression of the suit, ought to be clear. We have become saddled with such burdens through sheer lack of insight. We have often acted without thought, being ripe for the challenge, and now everything has become too much. A close look at this card shows the figure on a path in the foreground (as with other cards in this suit – see the Nine and the Four). This is the person's own, true life path, from which he is about to stray (his left foot is poised to lead him away from it). In other words, the burden he is carrying does not really belong to him. He has taken on not only more than he can deal with, but more than is necessary. He

could, if he thought about it, drop the whole load at any time. Similarly, we can always, if we really try, work out a simpler way to solve our weighty problems.

**Key sentence for interpretation:** Oppression and burdens, perhaps mental or emotional, may prove to be self-imposed; it is time to let go and lighten our load.

## Page of Wands

A young man's attention has been caught by the stave he gently holds. He wears red tights and a red feather in his hat, the colour echoing the red landscape beyond him.

The Page cards all represent an early flowering of the energy associated with their suit. Something here is stirring into life. This is different from the Aces, where the new raw energy is already fully present. Pages refer to the child stage of development; they can refer to actual children, but generally symbolise youthfulness, innocence and vigour (that is only first channelled and contained in the Queens). In Wands, the Page stands for raw enthusiasm, represented by the card's dominant red colour, and the first shoots of creative imagination, symbolised by the small red feather, whether or not this is directed into constructive outlets. As such, this energy may surface merely as the restless desire for something new to happen, even if we aren't sure what that something is supposed to be.

**Key sentence for interpretation:** This is a time of psychic and spiritual exploration characterised by imagination, innocence and vigour.

## Knight of Wands

A knight in bright clothes on the back of galloping red horse holds his wand aloft. Like the Page's, his tunic is bright yellow and is decorated with salamanders.

The Knight is in the same red landscape (with its pyramid-like hills) as the Page, although he is not at rest but passing swiftly through. This is the key to the image, for the Knight is volatile and changeable, unable to stay in one place for very long. Knights generally symbolise the speed, energy and adaptability of late youth (from adolescence to approaching maturity), and with Fire the Knight is full of new ideas, optimism, excitement and hopes for the future. In all, this adds up to a sense of idealism and adventure, a thirst for change, and the desire to seek out a new life and broaden our horizons, mentally or physically. Sometimes the appearance of this card coincides with such changes in a quite literal sense, indicating that a house move or other change of environment is a present consideration.

**Key sentence for interpretation:** Change is in the air; there is a mood of expansion, energy and adaptability.

## Queen of Wands

A stately queen on her throne is surrounded by symbols of Fire: two Egyptian lions, a huge sunflower, a wand, a royal cat and, behind her head, a lion motif.

The woman's bearing here indicates both pride and self-confidence,

qualities resulting from the combination of Wands/Fire and the stabilising quality of the Queen card. She has the vigour and fiery enthusiasm of the other court Wands, but here these energies are powerfully contained and channelled. Her sunny nature and love for life are represented in the emblems around her. The feline animals symbolise both her passion for life and her strong and indomitable will. All of the Queens have this sustainable strength; here, the power is one of joy, inner confidence and magnanimity, together with the strength of personality that comes from a forceful spirit. We may be about to meet with such qualities, whether in ourselves or in others.

**Key sentence for interpretation:** We may feel a love of life and a sense of inner confidence and strength; we are creative and our will is now strong.

## King of Wands

A red-gowned king sits upon a throne decorated with silhouettes of salamanders and lions. The same design covers his cloak. A salamander appears at his feet.

While the Queen sits in confident repose, the King seems poised for action. This is an image about the pure energy of Wands directed towards manipulating the environment. The King holds a staff in his right hand (for willed action), because he may be called upon at any moment to right wrongs on behalf of his people. All the Kings have this connotation of responsibility, of being a higher authority and someone on whom others rely. The Kings are also strategists who change things in the prevailing social order. They improve the status quo if possible, and here the enthusiasm and vision of Wands combines with a display of leadership and authority. The salamander is the alchemist's totem beast of fire, a symbol of spiritual rebirth. The King of Wands

lives only for his noble vision of how life ought to be, the ideal as opposed to the real with all its imperfections. Thus we meet with qualities of honesty, idealism, forthrightness, optimism, courage and loyalty – but also impatience!

**Key sentence for interpretation:** This is a time of responsibility, authority and leadership; we may be ambitious in our work and may experience a sense of courage, idealism and impatience.

## Chapter 6
# The Minor Arcana –
# the Suit of Cups

The suit of Cups is associated with Water, representing love, relationships and intuition, as well as the cycle of life, from birth to death and rebirth.

## Ace of Cups

Here we see a left hand emerging from a cloud, bearing a large golden chalice overflowing with water, which replenishes the pool below. The whole scene resembles an ever-flowing fountain. The holy dove brings a wafer from heaven to place in the cup.

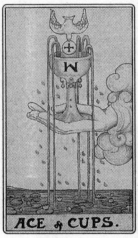

With its strong suggestions of the Holy Grail and the grace (forgiveness) of God, this deeply symbolic card is primarily about the realm of the feelings and their workings. Emotions have their own kind of logic when the heart guides the way, and, of course, they play a major role in the sphere of personal relationships. In a spread this card signifies a new situation that is emotionally charged, one to which our hearts are open and in which we are thus able to express our true feelings. The image on this card is almost perfectly symmetrical. Thus it often indicates a time of balance in our life (when nothing is upsetting our sense of emotional security) and of abundant feeling. With its fruitful quality, the Ace of Cups can sometimes indicate a pregnancy.

**Key sentence for interpretation:** The feelings have been awakened; this is a period of emotional growth and readiness to explore the heart, possibly indicating a new love relationship.

## Two of Cups

A motif of a lion's head and a pair of wings appears to hover protectively over a pair of young lovers, who each bear a large chalice. Between them is a caduceus – two snakes entwined around a vertical column.

With its alchemical emblems (the lion symbolises the potentially perfect union of male and female) and dynamic symmetry (since the figures are in the act of exchanging cups), this image is one of active relationship and balance. Everything here suggests exchange, give and take; what happens in one half of the picture is complemented by what happens in the other. The male figure is colourfully dressed in a red headband and passes the cup to his partner with his left hand; the female is dressed plainly and uses her right hand. With balance and interaction, there is the potential for a near perfect relationship, just so long as this dynamic give and take continues. This card thus signifies the potential for harmonious new friendship, a love affair or even a business arrangement.

**Key sentence for interpretation:** There is friendly and harmonious co-operation in partnerships of all kinds, but especially in matters of the heart.

## *Three of Cups*

Three women raise their cups aloft in a gesture of joyous celebration. Abundant fruit lies at their feet.

The image here speaks quite plainly for the most part. It is about celebrating things of the heart, whether this is a newly begun love

affair, some happy family news or a much desired new job. Something has brought fulfilment and there is an occasion to celebrate. The happiness is such that we wish to share it others. The ripe fruit lying around speaks of the fruition of what we've been conceiving or creating recently. Now there is success. There is also a more subtle meaning here – about the open-hearted trust we show in life and others. Here is the real reason for the celebration in the card; our faith alone has vindicated us. The extent to which we truly believe the good things of life are on their way is the extent to which they readily appear!

**Key sentence for interpretation:** There is a sense of emotional reward and fulfilment, in which matters come to fruition, usually – though not always – in love.

## Four of Cups

A bored young man, his arms folded, sits beneath a tree staring at three cups lined up before him. A spectral hand presents him with a fourth cup, which he fails to notice.

Unlike its predecessor, this card has glum connotations. The happiness of the Three has reached its zenith and there is no further joy to be had, so dissatisfaction and boredom follow. Clearly, this is a critical stage. Either something must be revitalised or our thoughts must turn to dramatically changing our circumstances. This kind of apathy is often the result of our having had too much of a good thing and needing to be shaken out of our complacency. The cup being offered from 'outside' is really our better self reminding us that our thought habits are making the situation seem much worse than it really is. The single cup is significant: a cup on its own is an ace, and aces are about the potential for emotional enjoyment. In other words, we need to go back and discover what it was about our situation that first brought us pleasure. We have not lost anything yet.

**Key sentence for interpretation:** Personal happiness may have turned stale; a current situation may offer ongoing security but little excitement.

## Five of Cups

Under a grey sky, a solemn, black-cloaked figure lowers his head, while before him a river rushes on beneath a bridge. Five cups are arranged around him, three of them upturned, their contents spilled on the ground.

With its visual cliché of the cup of joy overturned, this card is not

difficult to understand. This is inverted happiness, the love that cannot now be contained in the matrix of a stable relationship. The pain and withdrawal, the regret and disappointment here are palpable. However, the symbolic bridge and the two standing cups suggest a kind of way through, indicating that at least something can be done to deal with the debris of the situation. The remaining two cups symbolise hope (the Two of Cups is about potential relationship), for no matter how deeply we have suffered emotionally, there is always hope that our life can be rebuilt. The bridge, however, can only be crossed and the city reached when the loss has been fully accepted. The figure here is

still too immersed in his melancholy to cross that bridge to a new phase of life. This card warns us not to dwell too deeply on our losses. Just as the river flows in eternal motion, so we cannot arrest our feelings. We must accept the lows along with the highs and get on with life.

**Key sentence for interpretation:** There may be feelings of regret and disappointment over a loss of some kind but we must not allow this to hold us back from other objectives.

## Six of Cups

Two children are at play, surrounded by high-walled buildings. The scene contains six cups, each of them containing a white flower.

If we look at this card as the next stage in the overall process of the Cups suit, the sadness of the Five has been replaced by the simplicity and innocence of happy memories, upon which we now build the future. The key to the Six of Cups is in its symbols of the past, and the things we can rely on to bring pleasure. We return, in some sense, to a less complicated phase of our life, whether through memory or some actual connection to people from our past – parents, friends or brothers and sisters. Here is what once made us feel secure. At a deep level, we are looking for that inner child, that uncomplicated side of us that is free to express itself with joy – a side that was nurtured most in childhood. To think of this card in terms of pure nostalgia would be a mistake; what is happening here is a far more dynamic process. This

card speaks of how the past relates in a significant way to what we are doing now.

**Key sentence for interpretation:** This is a time of serene passage through life due to some inward happiness linked to the past; we reassess our life through our roots, and the past comes alive again in some way.

## Seven of Cups

A figure is in shadow, bedazzled by a seductive vision that issues from a cloud: seven cups bearing a snake, a woman's face, a veiled figure, a laurel wreath, jewels, a castle and a lizard.

These visions represent the hopes and fears of humanity in general,

and this card shows how easy it is for us to be carried away by an over-active imagination. Since the cups mostly refer to matters of the heart, this card is quite often about the ways in which we idealise certain situations in love. Sometimes we are carried away by fantasies of the perfect love even before any relationship actually exists. This card usually describes a situation where we need to be careful in making choices in love. The challenge is to not let the heart rule the head completely, although that is easier said than done. We can all delude ourselves, and the pull of certain emotions is indeed difficult to resist, but until anything in our particular situation is more concrete, we should be careful. Our head may be in the clouds, but that doesn't have to stop us from having our feet on the ground.

**Key sentence for interpretation:** We may be in danger of self-delusion regarding a current situation or relationship and must exercise caution in making particular choices.

## Eight of Cups

In this nocturnal scene a red-robed figure leaves behind the arrangement of eight cups we see in the foreground. An alchemical moon seems to be swallowing the sun.

This card is closely related to the Five, but there are significant differences. The figure is no longer pre-occupied with his feelings. His robe has changed from black to red (the active principle) and he has reached the other bank of the river – in gaining dry land he actively takes charge of his life. With this card we leave behind certain feelings that have in one sense become useless to us. We have realised the futility of regret and no longer wish to carry around the past. Thus, unlike the Five, this card can indicate a renunciation of a current phase of life (usually a relationship) that no longer fulfils us. The peculiar, asymmetrical arrangement of the standing cups indicates that there may be something missing in our life when this card appears – usually, a sense of emotional fulfilment. The swallowed sun emblem suggests that our creativity and happiness may currently be lacking and signifies a sense of gloom. Nevertheless, there is resignation to the present reality as we accept all that is necessary.

**Key sentence for interpretation:** Ties to the past are willingly, if somewhat regretfully, cut; we let go and move on so that major change can eventually take place.

## Nine of Cups

A red-capped male figure sits complacently as if at a feast, his arms folded in satisfaction. Before him nine goblets are arranged in a crescent moon formation.

Wherever we see almost perfect symmetry in a Tarot image we can

be sure that there is allusion to some kind of harmony and fulfilment. The man's head is precisely in the middle of horizontal axis of the card, and the central chalice appears directly above his head; thus everything on his left and right appears to be in perfect equilibrium. Usually associated with transient pleasures, this card really indicates that a sense of psychological balance and receptivity is what actually brings emotional satisfaction, as well as outward reward. No matter how much the world outside loses its head, if we maintain our poise and peace of mind, no situation on earth can really disturb our inner security and contentment. This is because we are always approaching life from a position of equilibrium, being centred enough in ourselves to handle whatever life puts our way in a happy calm manner.

**Key sentence for interpretation:** This is a time of inner harmony, and a general sense of satisfaction and well-being are present, whether or not related to external circumstances.

## *Ten of Cups*

A vision of ten dazzling cups in rainbow formation is greeted with wondrous joy by a couple whose two children dance ecstatically nearby.

Since the numbered cards can all be seen as part of gradual process, the Ten of Cups, with its simple pleasures of familial contentment, follows logically after the lessons of the Eight and the final attainment of happiness in the Nine. The Ten perfects what was begun in the Nine. We have moved from a state of emotional balance to a spontaneous outpouring of joy, symbolised by the innocent children. We have moved from the Nine's sense of inward contentment to the more outward aspects of the search for fulfilment – hence the happy family and secure environment. Indeed, such is often indicated when the Ten of Cups appears. Generally, though, this card refers to any emotional situation that brings satisfaction and happiness, and often appears when a personal relationship is doing just that. The gesture

made by the parents as they greet the appearance of the rainbow shows that they recognise well the value of simple joy and the ability to let go and enjoy what life has to offer.

**Key sentence for interpretation:** A situation in our life is accompanied by joy, security and a reason to celebrate.

## Page of Cups

A young page lifts a chalice, out of which a fish appears. He stands on dry land, but just behind him the sea is gently rising and falling.

The young man appears not even to notice the fish (symbolising the potential wisdom of intuitions), which nevertheless gazes at him.

Though standing on solid ground, he is poised on the shore of the imagination, which so often contains distracting fantasies. The turquoise (for deep feeling) of the fish, the sea and even his apparel dominate the image. Here is the young – perhaps adolescent – person first encountering certain emotions. Such feelings are at a rather inchoate and embryonic stage and are often dealt with awkwardly or may even be totally repressed, but this burgeoning of the feeling life must be gently encouraged. In fact, we can undergo this experience at any time in our life, for this card is often really about connecting (or rather reconnecting) to certain emotions, perhaps our ability to love and express affection after having been previously hurt in some manner. It is time to allow ourselves to feel.

PAGE of CUPS.

**Key sentence for interpretation:** We are sensitive and sympathetic to others; the emphasis is on feelings.

## Knight of Cups

A young knight with winged heels and helmet rides through an open landscape. His horse stoops, perhaps to drink from the stream they are approaching.

The active and freedom-loving quality of the Knights fits well with the element of Water, or suit of Cups, but with Cups the activity is mostly in the imagination, the realm of the heart and romantic ideals. The wings on the Knight's head and feet show his need to take flight, while his white horse looks passively downwards to the watery depths. Here is the key to the inner conflict represented by the Knight of Cups: he tends to avoid true self-analysis, insight and reflection, preferring to dream and stay under the spell of his illusions. The Knight of Cups can signify a lack of true action and commitment to the world, for the dream may be spoilt by having to deal with the limitations of the real world; much better to keep things in their perfect state, in the imagination. Even so, his romanticism, charm, grace and sensitivity are attractive and even noble qualities; we may be about to meet with them in someone, or find them in ourselves.

**Key sentence for interpretation:** We may be feeling romantic and imaginative, but we should guard against losing ourselves in illusions.

123

## Queen of Cups

A queen sits on the seashore upon an ornate throne. She peers intently at an even more ornate-looking cup, gaudily designed with arms and crescent moons.

The Queen is the only figure among the Cups court cards to give any

real attention to the cup that each holds. The other three – male – figures are, in some sense, avoiding the deeper realms of feeling thus symbolised (or having to get to grips with other issues at the same time). However, the fixity and stability of the Queen here ensures that emotional development is of prime importance. She knows that there is a possibility of great empowerment in feeling. This is not the wishy-washy romanticism of the Knight; rather, she is able to commit to life with the full force of her passions and to handle human situations with real emotional maturity guided by her strong intuitions. Like the Queen of Pentacles, she focuses her energies in one area in a powerful way,

QUEEN of CUPS.

so becoming determined and reliable. Likewise, her feelings are deep and constant, and never superficial. When this card appears we may encounter someone (possibly a woman) who is rather enigmatic, intuitive and even sexy – but, as with all the court cards, remember that these qualities could be awaiting development within ourselves.

**Key sentence for interpretation:** We are attaining emotional maturity in some sense, possibly through nurturing others.

## King of Cups

On a scallop-backed throne sits a sombre-looking king. Behind him (on the left) a ship sails. On his right, a fish jumps out of the water.

The King here seems somehow confined, his throne surrounded on all sides by choppy seas, while he is covered with symbols of the feeling world (his turquoise garment, his fish-scaled shoes). The image of a throne arising from the sea is unnatural, indicating that the King wears his feelings in a rather awkward way. The masculine authority and power of the King, in other words, blends uneasily with the passivity and emotion represented by Cups. Although he has sympathy and compassion in abundance and is sensitive and creative, the King of Cups is shy about expressing his true feelings. This may become a problem if certain emotions are repressed. The watery symbolism surrounding the King shows how very close he is to rather powerful, raw emotions – he is especially attuned to childhood and the past. And yet

at the same time these emotions frighten him. As a result, he has pursued accomplishments that express his innate creativity or artistic bent, or has turned to helping others on the emotional level. The King of Cups is imaginative, caring and secretly romantic. When he appears in a spread we may meet someone like this, or find the qualities in ourselves.

**Key sentence for interpretation:** There is an emotional receptivity but also a fear of feeling; support and protection may be a theme.

# Chapter 7
# The Minor Arcana – the Suit of Swords

The suit of Swords relates to Air. It is concerned with logic and determination, courage, the male principle and the mind.

## Ace of Swords

A right hand appears out of a cloud, firmly grasping a sword whose tip pierces a golden crown draped with laurel.

All the Aces in the Waite deck are illustrated with this mysterious hand-from-the-cloud motif, which stands for something new being

presented to the individual, a new content or energy arising in our consciousness, as if from out of the blue. In the suit of Swords, we are in the realm of pure thought, intellect, ideas and the cutting edge of the mind itself. We may speak, for example, of the sword of truth, for it is only in getting to grips with the bare, cold facts of existence that any awareness can arise. So this card is often about the emergence not simply of new ideas and plans, but also of a new way of seeing things, a new realisation, as our awareness expands and new truths dawn. When this card appears in a spread, it is time to be honest with ourselves and with others. This may upset things for a while as old illusions are dispelled and other people realise that they are dealing with our changed attitudes, but there is a chance for refreshing new viewpoints to emerge. Laurel wreaths typically symbolise victory; here, this is the victory of clarity and truth over illusion.

**Key sentence for interpretation:** A new awareness may emerge into the light of day, bringing an end to ignorance or uncertainty.

## Two of Swords

A blindfolded woman dressed in white sits on a stone plinth under a crescent moon in a dusky sky. Behind her is a calm sea and low hills in the distance. She crosses her arms in a death pose, holding a sword pointing to heaven in each hand.

The posture here is one of having withdrawn from conflict; the woman's arms form a protective cross over her body. Since Swords represent the realm of ideas, the Two (duality, opposition) refers to mental stasis and stalemate, where conflicting views cancel each other out. This may be between oneself and others, or internally, where we are divided on an issue. Usually it is easier to keep the peace by saying nothing, but this card warns that we should face certain situations openly. The implication is that we have blindfolded ourselves to the present truth, and the crossed swords represent our protection from unpalatable facts. But (depending on the surrounding cards) this is not the only interpretation. In times of conflict, it can symbolise a positive situation: the stalemate where neither side gets the upper hand, or a truce. The Two of Swords may appear at times when we need to go within and achieve an internal balance, to be centred and detached from warring forces around us.

**Key sentence for interpretation:** This is a period of enforced balance, when the forces of opposition are held in check; we may avoid conflict by withdrawing from the fray or simply stand our ground.

## Three of Swords

Beneath storm clouds in the middle of a downpour of rain, a heart is pierced by three swords.

The holding pattern of the Two card has broken down here; the two opposing forces can no longer remain as they were, and storm clouds

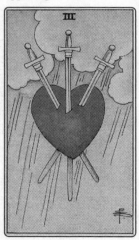

now break as the tension is finally released. There is an obvious sense of overarching pain and sadness here. As with the Five of Cups, there is a feeling of loss, hurt and separation. But whereas the powerful identification with sadness in the Five of Cups may require that we be gentle with ourselves and allow ourselves time to heal, the Three of Swords requires much less introspection. Swords are an active, discriminatory experience, and when this card appears we may have to realise that any attachment to pain is now destructive and must be released. The image on the card is brutal. Whatever may have ended in our lives we must now relinquish on an emotional level, and the sooner the better, for we may be preventing something new from appearing. This is a card of strife and conflict, to be sure, but the decks must cleared for new action. The temporary upheaval will be worth the trouble in the long run.

**Key sentence for interpretation:** We may be undergoing the pain of upheaval and discord; as much as possible, we must willingly separate ourselves from it in order for our overall situation improve.

## Four of Swords

A still figure lies prone inside a church, his hands arranged in a gesture of supplication. Above him are three swords, while a fourth (his own) is represented in a carving on the side of his tomb.

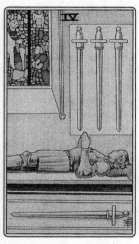

The man here is probably a Templar knight, one of the Knights of Christ, who may or may not be dead in the picture. However, the pose and gesture are what's important. The theme here is of rest, stillness, repose and recuperation following the exhaustive strife of the Three. But there are deeper connotations, for the stained glass window above the figure shows an individual receiving a blessing from Christ. The theme here is of healing or wholeness, for it is only when we have withdrawn and truly let go of conflict and trouble that the forces of the unconscious can take over and begin the renewal process. Thus, this is not merely a card of retreat from the hurly-burly of the world, but one of real (even spiritual) strength regained. This can only be achieved by letting go completely of our worldly cares and concerns.

**Key sentence for interpretation:** We may be experiencing a peaceful, introverted phase in life; there may be chance to heal and recuperate following a time of unrest; we gather strength slowly now.

## Five of Swords

A grinning figure looks on victorious as his defeated enemies retreat from the battlefield. He is holding three swords, and a further two in his possession are laid nearby.

Here is the image not of mere hostility, but of total defeat. The

intimidation is mirrored in the rough sea and the menacing, jagged sky on the horizon. Here it seems as if the whole world is against us, and when the Five of Swords appears in a spread we are quite often in the midst of a phase where nothing seems to go right. This is not an uncommon experience, and all we can do is realise our present limitations and make the best of things. The only consolation is that if the world really is having its way with you, the present state of affairs probably can't get any worse. The attitude required here is one of self-honesty and realism. The Five of Swords is one of the more overtly 'negative' cards, but once we have fully accepted our situation, at least life can get moving once again. This may be a depressing and humiliating time – two of this card's traditional keywords are defeat and dishonour – but time eventually passes and the cycle moves on.

**Key sentence for interpretation:** We seem to be defeated, either by life in general or someone in particular, and should accept our losses and prepare to think ahead.

## Six of Swords

A young ferryman steers a boat over calm waters towards a distant shore. His passengers are two hooded figures: a mother and child. In the boat stand six upright swords.

This card, with its sense of the relaxed and peaceful, seems almost a remedy for the sense of loss and defeat we saw in the Five, but we are not quite there yet. What is suggested here is the experience of gentle passage, of healing, of being calmer within so as to deal with our problems. Notice how, even though the image evokes serene progress, the boat is nonetheless burdened by its six heavy swords – wouldn't the journey be easier without them? The point is that composure and inner stillness makes the burden of problems that much easier to bear. Troublesome situations are less of a bother when we have a balanced mind and an understanding heart. The contents of the boat symbolise the contents of the psyche itself – thoughts and feelings –

under the guidance of the greater will, which is guiding the vessel with quiet certainty to its destination. Look, too, at how the Swords are arranged, in a group of two and four – balance and peace. Our own internal balance at this time keeps us on an even keel.

**Key sentence for interpretation:** There is gentle passage, often away from a phase of conflict and towards a calmer resolution of an issue; there may be a more balanced understanding of previous matters too.

## Seven of Swords

A young man, grinning with satisfaction, is stealing away from an enemy camp carrying five swords, while a further two remain upright in the ground.

This is another path card in which things are about to become

unbalanced; compare it to the Ten of Wands. The figure carries off five swords, which may imply a dangerously self-defeating act (remember what the Five of Swords means) and leaves two behind (balance). Seven in numerology is often ambiguous; certainly it has little to do with direct willed action; thus this card is about indirect actions – dishonesty, trickery, subterfuge or the simpler tactics of slippery diplomacy and wiliness. The rest of the image tends to confirm this: the man leads with his left (indirect, passive) foot on the path and appears to know precisely what he is doing, despite the potential danger. Note the yellow background; yellow symbolises awareness – there is forethought here. A plan is being executed and the tactics are subtle ones. A little craftiness and cunning will serve our ends far better than open confrontation when this card appears in a spread.

**Key sentence for interpretation:** We may be better off using wit, guile and secretive means in pursuit of our aims, rather than more outward, obvious tactics.

## Eight of Swords

A young woman stands blindfolded in a muddy field; her arms are bound with cloth. Around her eight tall swords are stuck into the ground. A huge castle stands in the background.

In spite of the imprisoning and humiliating elements of this image, what is really confining us here is ourselves. Notice how there is almost nothing to constrain the apparently unfortunate woman; the cloth that binds her does not seem terribly effective, and she could wriggle free with a little effort. Even the ground is relatively dry, or the swords could not stand. In fact, though outer circumstance has apparently conspired to bring about this sense of restriction in the Eight of Swords, our resistance is stronger than we think, which may be the general situation if this card appears in a spread. The Five of Swords is the card of utter defeat; here there is greater self-awareness with regard to the situation, and we often (like the woman in the picture) have the

means to free ourselves. This card may turn up when the individual is faced with a tough decision and is afraid to make it because of possible negative repercussions. We dealt with the situation with tact and cunning in the Seven; now we must face things openly. The time for helplessness is over – throw off the restraints and take action.

**Key sentence for interpretation:** We may feel hampered by circumstance, afraid to act – but act we must, with courage and honesty.

## Nine of Swords

A woman sits up in bed weeping, her head in her hands. Behind her, in the darkness, we see nine horizontal swords. Her bedclothes are emblazoned with roses, zodiac signs and planetary glyphs.

Deep anxiety pervades this image. If we compare it with the Four of

Swords we will see that although three vertical swords seem to hang over the knight, he is protected from their apparent threat by his repose. Here, the woman sits up, facing the same direction as the swords against the same gloomy backdrop. We could interpret this as going with the flow of anxiety, letting our worries deepen and our imagination work overtime. The woman buries her face in fear; perhaps if she opened her eyes and questioned the meaning of the nine swords she would deal with the situation differently. She would see that our problems are of our own making, that worry begets worry and makes life even worse, but that fear is a fact of life and we must learn to live with

it. This means that we can still feel afraid in certain situations, but without letting fear rule our every move. Just as the woman hides her eyes from the swords, she likewise fails to notice the red (life, passion) roses, or the green (growth) glyphs. With a change of attitude, her eyes could be opened and she would see a different reality.

**Key sentence for interpretation:** We may be operating through fear and worry and need to face reality; our anxieties may be unfounded.

## Ten of Swords

A dead male figure lies on the ground under thick black skies, the horizon nevertheless retaining some brightness. Ten swords pierce his back.

This apparently fatal and disastrous image seems to point to matters being even worse than we encountered in the Nine; however, they are in fact better, or at least not quite as awful as they seem. This is made plain by the yellow light in the background. We might ask whether the light is fading or dawning. The answer is either. The idea of transition from one mental or emotional reality to another is indicated. If the light is diminishing then at least the blackness will soon come to an end; day must eventually follow night – another way of saying that things cannot get any worse. The traditional interpretation, however, is that the worst is already over, that the background light is encroaching. It is dawn and our worries are spent. If we think of this image as purely symbolic – a death or an ending to the situation in the previous card – then this is the absolute end of an anxious circumstance.

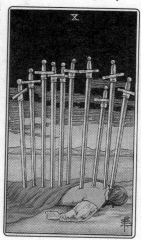

**Key sentence for interpretation:** A worrying situation is coming to an end, or has ended, and new attitudes can finally be adopted as we face the future.

## Page of Swords

A young man lifts his sword in a distracted manner. He is pictured, as it were, with his head in the clouds, while birds fly overhead.

Here we see much that symbolises the free spirit of the element of Air. When this card appears there may be embryonic ideas that we

must absorb and develop for ourselves. The Page symbolises the emergence of new mental faculties, perhaps through new intellectual interests, or the birth of fresh attitudes and ways of thinking in relation to a current situation. But these are early days, for thinking and learning are not the same as understanding. While proper insight and wisdom are lacking, it may be that mere curiosity will do. At this stage of development, such mental detachment means that we are at least free to change our mind and entertain different points of view, for no fixed vision has manifested. Sometimes this playful, trivial attitude manifests negatively as childish and gossipy comments about others. But this card represents in essence a quality of inquisitiveness and the desire for input of all kinds as we become fascinated by certain aspects of the world.

**Key sentence for interpretation:** At this time we may develop a new interest and will feel generally inquisitive about the world.

## Knight of Swords

In strong winds, a knight charges towards his destination, his sword held aloft beneath a jagged sky.

A far more direct figure than the Page, the Knight stands for all that is swift, changeable, clever and articulate; he embodies the ability to quickly grasp a situation with the mind and then move on (though he has little emotional depth). As with any court card, these traits may be within us, or we may meet them in people currently at large in our lives. Here, then, is a mercurial and changeable type of person, but the real key to this image is its speed, for it is the agility of his thoughts, his lightning wit and his versatile intellect that characterise the Knight. His fast-moving energies and impatience may also mean a swift change to the old order of our life or some aspect of it. There are new ideas to be put into action, and the Knight says, 'The sooner, the better.' Such a situation may be present when the Knight of Swords appears in a spread.

Key sentence for interpretation: We may experience swift changes but will have the mental agility and versatile intellect to cope.

## Queen of Swords

A queen sits on a throne with scrolled features, a raised sword in her right hand. A tassel hangs from her left arm, which is raised, perhaps to bless someone.

The Queen holds the only Sword in the court cards that is held aloft

in a perfectly vertical position. It symbolises pure, upright and impartial judgement. It also stands for emotional detachment from a human situation. In traditional card interpretations this is because of some sorrow the Queen has at one time undergone. The position she now adopts is one seemingly above lowly human matters, with her head held high. She is the only court Queen who gazes off into the distance – her aloof posture also symbolises the mental distance from the world that is required in order to analyse, conceptualise, raise up and develop the intellect. Here, then, is someone who may keep the world of feelings at bay so they do not impinge, but here also are characteristics of independence, idealism, honesty, self-reliance, steadfastness and general loyalty to others – if they have earned it!

**Key sentence for interpretation:** We may be feeling independent and self-reliant; idealism and loyalty are also current themes.

## King of Swords

A king looks impassively out at the world, his sword lifted in his right hand. Behind him is the butterfly motif that also appeared in the Queen and Knight cards.

The King of Swords is a very different creature from the Queen. The sword is tilted slightly this time and appears in the right hand. If the Queen's upright, left-hand sword means impartiality and passivity (as the human world passes 'beneath' her), then the King's right-hand sword shows that he is more actively involved. He wilfully engages with what is out there. He has the quality of intellect and reason, like the other court Swords, but here it is far more dynamic. He represents the rational principle as applied to the human world, hence matters such as fairness, equality, justice and democracy in action, and being a King, he demonstrates leadership in this sphere. His finely wrought intellect makes him a teacher of sorts, or at least a figure of wise counsel.

**Key sentence for interpretation:** We may find ourselves actively involved in issues of justice, in which intellect and reason must be brought to bear.

# Chapter 8
# The Minor Arcana – the Suit of Pentacles

Pentacles relate to the Earth element, representing order in all areas, natural and man-made, as well as the home, family and security.

## Ace of Pentacles

A right hand appears from a heavenly cloud bearing a dazzling Pentacle. Below is a richly fecund, hedged garden, whose exit beyond the walls leads to mountains in the far distance.

To begin on a rather esoteric note, this card depicts the point where

the spiritual plane meets the earthly; that is, where our dreams are at last beginning to become real, where our inner vision of the future is actually beginning to take shape. When this card appears, specific plans may still be largely unformed and anything can happen, but the promise is now there for material success. New finance and possessions may not be long in coming our way. This is usually because whatever path we has been taking have led to new opportunities or even some significant good luck. There is now a general feeling of contentment and a new faith in the future. This card suggests getting off to a promising start on a practical level.

**Key sentence for interpretation:** There may be new material beginnings or an opportunity to increase financial resources; the physical dimension of life is generally enjoyable.

## Two of Pentacles

A juggler with two coins is depicted within the lemniscate – a figure-of-eight halo – of the Magician. A ship in the distance negotiates a rather choppy sea.

This image is about movement, both literal and metaphorical. Just as the coins the juggler manipulates are about  to change hands, so this card suggests that money must change hands if our material plans are to succeed. This may mean taking risks with investment, being open to monetary fluctuations and having some foresight when planning ahead. Quite often a figurative juggling of resources is required as – like the ship in this image – we try to navigate the road ahead. This card requires us to be less influenced by material demands, to enjoy the game of life, and especially to be flexible and play with the cycles of change that are occurring throughout our material universe when it appears in a spread.

**Key sentence for interpretation:** In order to succeed at the material level we should pay attention to financial fluctuations and be adaptable and ready to take risks – the forces of change are in operation.

## *Three of Pentacles*

A mason completes work on an archway, presumably in a monastery; two other figures, a monk and an architect, inspect the work. Above their heads, within a gothic arch, are three pentacles arranged in a triangle.

This is an image of productivity and skilful creation, which is nevertheless guided by more authoritative figures who should soon reward our efforts. But the monk (spirituality) and the architect (mental skills) are of course symbolic – they belong to us too. They suggest a higher principle associated with work: one that leads to excellence, great satisfaction and even self-discovery. On a broader level this card is about right action, about following the correct course of all things, and ultimately about mastering the skills of life itself. Thus, it is no surprise that it often appears in a spread when an early material success is indicated in a situation where our gifts are put to use, often with some appreciation and encouragement from influential people.

**Key sentence for interpretation:** Mastering certain skills may lead to financial reward; there may be early material successes that promise much for the future.

## Four of Pentacles

A regal, male figure holds on to a pentacle; beneath each of his feet and above his head are more pentacles. While on one level the figure seems secure and happily at rest, at the same time there is a sense of apprehension, as if he is unable to let go of what he is holding.

However, the figure could equally well be in the act of rotating the coin in his arms, suggesting an intuition of the cyclical nature of the universe (money comes and goes; our bank balance moves – whether we like it or not – up and down). Here is the real lesson of this card: that our attachments to money and possessions may be the hidden cause of future losses. While, on the one hand, our affairs may be fairly stable, there may at the same time be little room for change or growth, and stagnation is the result. Sometimes this card appears in spreads where the querent is thriftily getting by or is enforcing economic cutbacks. There may be personal security here, but we may also be over-attached to the symbols of that security. The man in the image must allow that coin to turn – allow money to move around, to flow – and not be afraid of spending. This card is often associated with miserliness.

**Key sentence for interpretation:** Despite our financial security, we may be clinging on too tightly to the material universe and thus preventing future growth.

## Five of Pentacles

Two figures in threadbare clothes, one of them lame, suffer the cold of a nocturnal snowstorm as they pass beneath a stained glass window featuring five pentacles. The lame figure looks up at this.

The Scrooge-like approach suggested in the Four has turned into

need and poverty in the Five. One of the *bêtes noires* of the Minor Arcana, because of its association with insecurity, hardship and loss of money, this card – for most people – has no redeeming features at all. When it appears, either hardship is by now a fact of life or the way ahead looks rather threadbare. In the first instance the only thing to do is accept the situation and try to move on, yet there is a lesson to be learned here. The larger situation is telling us that the material world is never quite as secure as we choose to think and cannot be relied upon. Everything is subject to change. Perhaps the impoverishment shown in the card is a result of not preparing carefully enough for the future;

perhaps the situation comes out of the blue. At any rate, we must go beyond any sense of loss and learn to let go of it. Perhaps then the necessary changes can come along a little quicker

**Key sentence for interpretation:** This a time of material hardship and financial problems, which may have resulted from pride and ignorance – it may be time for a change of attitude.

## Six of Pentacles

A wealthy, finely dressed merchant weighs coins with a pair of scales and hands out measured amounts to the figures kneeling at his feet.

This is apparently an image of benevolent charity, but the Six of Pentacles has complex psychological meanings. It is a card about the nature of both giving and receiving. The standing figure is handing out what he knows the others can use, or what they are able (according to their station in life) to receive. Thus it says as much about the nature of those on the receiving end as it does about the giver, for much in human nature resists so-called charity. The kneeling figures, however, (unlike those in the Five) are now ready to receive material assistance; that is, they have put themselves in the correct position to be helped. But they have attracted only the amount of money that they believe they are worth; this is why the money must be measured out. This card suggests that munificence in the form of help from above is on its way,

usually because it has been well earned, though not necessarily through hard work. It is our faith in life and the world as an essentially benevolent place that has helped change things.

**Key sentence for interpretation:** Plentiful resources, usually financial, are made available, and we may well be on the receiving end; alternatively, we may be required to help others by a distribution of resources.

## Seven of Pentacles

A distressed-looking figure stares down with dissatisfaction at the work he has just completed.

This is an image of uncertainty and vacillation. When this card turns up in a spread, there may be stagnation if crucial alterations are not

 made to a work in progress or plan of action. In many ways this is a rethink period when we must consider whether or not to proceed on the same course. We may see the need for a change of tack – and much may depend on our decision. The seven coins the figure gazes at are arranged in no orderly fashion but require organising in a satisfactory and efficient way. This may be what our own lives need when this card appears. Often there is a practical decision to be made. We may be at the archetypal crossroads, or the material conditions may simply require better organising. What we have successfully built up in the past may no longer be working out and change is required if our better decisions are not to go awry through inaction and indecision.

**Key sentence for interpretation:** Changes and new decisions may be called for over a practical matter or project, for this is a crossroads period when a new direction may have to be taken.

## Eight of Pentacles

An obviously contented figure, caught up with the task in hand, puts the finishing touches to one of eight coins. A further coin waits on the floor, ready to be engraved.

The indecision and dissatisfaction suggested in the Seven have here turned into rewarding action, so much so that the apprentice-like figure is lost in the enjoyment of his task. In fact, the idea of the archetypal apprentice is more or less the key to this card, for the learning of new and necessary skills is not limited to our youth. At any time in life we may have to adapt to new circumstances that require us to absorb and master new ideas and to develop relevant skills. Such is the way real progress is made, as we attune ourselves to the workings of physical reality. When this card appears in a spread, the promise of reward for all of our labours is a reality. It represents a time when we have channelled our energies into improving skills and building on latent talents. This will soon pay off.

**Key sentence for interpretation:** We may have to extend our work efforts to produce surer success in the future, possibly through new means of self-improvement and the development of new skills.

# Nine of Pentacles

One of the more fortuitous Pentacles cards, the Nine (three times three equals creativity multiplied) depicts a finely robed woman, holding aloft a hunting bird. She is standing in a vineyard, whose ripe fruits and foliage are abundant.

A sense of satisfaction is the traditional interpretation of this card, but what about the card's symbolism? The falcon perched on the woman's gauntlet represents the flight of ideas and creative instincts; traditionally this bird is associated with the spiritual realm, or the soul-in-flight. Notice how the woman exudes care and respect for the bird, as if it were an extension of herself. Practical human intelligence and creative imagination have worked in combination to produce wealth and success, for the woman stands contentedly within the abundant garden, her right hand resting on the uppermost pentacle. Here, also, we see three symbolic triangular formations (the perfection of 'three-ness' suggesting harmony and flowing energy). In this card, a proper estimation of personal worth and one's capabilities has led to material success and the kind of deep satisfaction and reward that comes from creative effort. Good luck and right action have combined.

**Key sentence for interpretation:** We are enjoying material reward, fulfilment and success due to a positive sense of self-worth; what we value about ourselves on the inner level has become our physical reality.

## Ten of Pentacles

A couple and their child stand on the threshold of a walled city, beneath an arched gateway. In the foreground two white dogs wait at the feet of a richly attired old man.

Like its predecessor one of the happier Pentacles cards, the Ten also contains many layers of symbolism. It is clear that the old man is connected with the family as a symbol of ancestral roots, stability and tradition. He especially represents the wise man or even magician, and, indeed, is surrounded by magical signs, tools and symbols, all on the left-hand side of the picture. This is an allusion to the fact that the material universe is subject to often complex occult (invisible) laws, and the outward material stability and security enjoyed by the family is not to be taken for granted. The old man is a mysterious presence, a magical symbol for what has been created externally. He is the male counterpart of the woman from the Nine card (look at the vines on his robe).

Scholars of the Kabbalah will notice that the arrangement of the ten pentacles is in the thinly disguised form of a Tree of Life. In short, inner creates outer – we have seen in the Nine how feelings of self-worth (inner riches if you like) lead to actual wealth. The two white dogs (instinct) recognise the old man for who he really is – an emblem of magical wisdom who possesses the secret of wealth. This card is not just about the fruits of success but also about how we perpetuate material riches, especially what we bequeath and pass on to others in our families – hence the three generations pictured here. This card therefore suggests material security, and the protection and comfort that arises out of it

**Key sentence for interpretation:** We may have the means to capitalise on current successes and create financial security and material wealth.

PAGE of PENTACLES

## Page of Pentacles

A young man holds lightly on to a single pentacle before him, in fascination. At his feet, flowers begin to grow more abundant.

On one level, this image shows how fragile our grip is on the material world, and this may actually be the case in our lives when the Page of Pentacles appears – we may have little real economic power. The card speaks of preparing ourselves for the material journey ahead. This preparation may range from educating ourselves about the practical details of a new project to putting money aside to finance a particular scheme. These things involve much patience and perhaps certain sacrifices, for we may have to forego immediate gratification in order to look ahead in the larger scheme of things. They also require a measure of faith in the future, as we gradually assemble the necessary resources (mental or material) for whatever we are building for the future.

**Key sentence for interpretation:** This is a time of planning for the future; patience, faith and sacrifice may all be required.

## Knight of Pentacles

In a rural setting, a heavily armoured knight holds a single pentacle. He is mounted on a sturdy black horse (possibly a workhorse) and looks ahead into the far distance.

The image is one of stillness and steadfastness. Of all the Knights, the Knight of Pentacles has the only horse that is not in motion – for the general idea of the Knight is of agility and speed. Here, then, the Knight's usual qualities of movement are channelled into more practical and earthly matters, having to do with immediate necessity, duty, labour and attention to detail. He looks ahead with longing to the future, while knowing that he is for now at the service of the material plane. Each of the Court figures bears their Pentacle differently, signifying their distinctive approach to material matters. The Page barely holds on to his Pentacle at all, the Queen lovingly inspects the disk in her lap, and the King proudly yet lightly lifts his Pentacle to show the world, for here is

calm authority over the physical world. The Knight, however, holds his Pentacle with care, signifying a committed sense of duty and responsibility. He has a capacity for industry, an adaptability to change and a need to be useful. When this card appears, such traits may be about to manifest in our life, through another or possibly in ourselves.

**Key sentence for interpretation:** Duty and responsibility are to the forefront, but there is also a capacity to adapt.

## Queen of Pentacles

A Queen sits upon her throne in a glade-like setting, surrounded by rose blooms and lush vegetation. She is studying the pentacle held in her lap.

All Queens possess the characteristics of stability and fixity of

purpose; with pentacles, we are in the sphere of earthly practical matters, those issues that are most visibly 'real' and physical. The Queen here is a sensuous creature, in love with all things in the natural world. Her attention is quietly fixed on the Pentacle, and this can mean she tends to value only that which she can see and touch physically. As a result she may have difficulty with other, subtler, aspects of reality, such as the intuitive and intellectual worlds. Her gifts belong to the palpable, physical world of the senses, and she doesn't merely appreciate nature from afar, she glories in it, being very much a part of it. She is in touch with her body, and thus usually maintains good physical health. She is patient, prudent and determined, if perhaps slower to act than her Swords or Wands counterparts. She is also extremely stubborn. When this card appears, such traits may be about to come to the fore in our life, through another or possibly in ourselves.

**Key sentence for interpretation:** We are in touch with our senses, patient, prudent and perhaps also stubborn.

## King of Pentacles

A king sits outside his castle, lightly holding to a pentacle. His colourful robe is decorated with a motif of grapes, while the rear of his throne has carved bulls' heads.

Here is the very image of worldly satisfaction and contentment, not through sensual union with nature as with the Queen, but through having conquered the physical universe. This may mean the archetypal self-made successful businessman who now sits back to enjoy his achievements, or someone whose gift is for turning dreams into reality. Whenever this card appears in a spread, it signifies the presence in our life of a hard-working, authoritative, and usually independent and confident individual whose skill is in the world of business, and who quite often demonstrates some kind of leadership capacity. The Kings of all suits are both innovators and authorities; that is, they get things underway and then master the situation. The castle situated to the rear of

the King of Pentacles represents what he has carefully built in his life; indeed, his main purpose is to achieve something that will outlast his own life.

**Key sentence for interpretation:** We are feeling confident and independent; this is a time of leadership and achievement.

# Chapter 9
# Working with Tarot Spreads

It is now time to look more closely at the actual spreads – the way in which the cards are laid out. As we have already seen in the simple three-card spread, certain positions are assigned specific meanings – but do remember that our experience of past and present is not demarcated with a clear dividing line. Remember, too, that cards that turn up in any 'future' position must take their place within the overall context of the spread; in other words, what may happen tomorrow has its roots firmly grounded in today, for nothing ever happens in isolation. The goal in any reading is synthesis. This is certainly the key to successful reading of the cards – seeing the whole picture that has been drawn.

There is a sense in which the positions in a spread are, in fact, arbitrary, and the meaning we attach to them is mainly a matter of choice. Indeed, you may one day wish to create your own spreads. While you are getting started, though, it is probably easier to stick to the traditional rules.

We will begin by looking at three main types of spread, to learn about how they are formed and what each position in the spread means. The chapter concludes with two actual examples of Tarot spreads performed for clients who were ready to undergo significant life changes. These will help to illustrate just how Tarot readings connect with the specific facts of someone's life. Let's start by looking at the Celtic Cross, one of the most popular spreads in contemporary use.

## The Celtic Cross spread

Shuffle the cards thoroughly and the choose ten at random from the pack. Place these face down in a heap, so that your first card is the one at the bottom of the pile. Then lay out the cards as illustrated opposite, in the form of a cross, laying your first chosen card in position one.

### The meaning of the positions of the cards

The following section describes which facet of the overall situation each numbered position deals with.

**1 The significator, or matter:** As its name implies, this position refers to the present issue on both inner and outer levels. It points to the real heart of the matter.

**2 The crossing card:** The crossing card is laid horizontally on card one. Combined with the significator, it is what produces the present situation. It refers to something that crosses, or stands in, the individual's path, or that generates the kind of energy we are dealing with.

**3 The crown:** Also known as the 'crowning card', this represents what is above us at present – the situation that is apparent in our life, and perhaps to others also, for the crown tends to refer to an external or at least rather obvious matter.

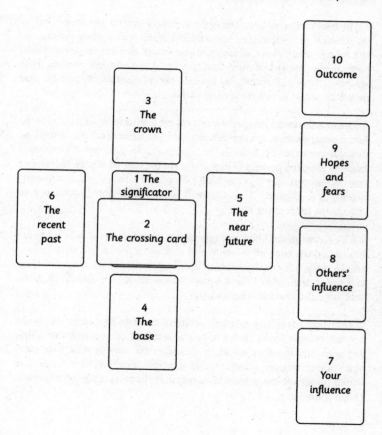

3
The
crown

10
Outcome

9
Hopes
and
fears

6
The
recent
past

1 The
significator

2
The crossing card

5
The
near
future

8
Others'
influence

4
The
base

7
Your
influence

**4 The base of the matter:** The opposite of the crown, the base is below us, which is to say that it refers to a hidden factor regarding the present situation – some inner, hitherto unsuspected element or unconscious part of the individual that has generated the current matter. It is whatever is at the source or core of the present circumstance, and makes its presence felt from deep within.

**5 The near future:** This card represents what is in front of us, and is the initial outgrowth of the present situation. In some cases this is the best possible outcome or, indeed, the only possible outcome if nothing is done to alter the present. Thus, it is a simple case of what's happening now manifesting itself as the future. But I stress that this is not already determined. If there is a negatively toned card here, take steps to change the present reality!

**6 The recent past:** This card represents what is behind us – what has influenced the current situation and in some sense caused what is now taking place. Obviously, the card here signifies what we can learn from and use in the future. Then it may be something we should dispense with for good and leave behind.

**7 Your influence:** This is a key position; it refers to a situation in the not too distant future that will be the result of our current input into our own life. In other words, it describes the way in which we have been influencing the situation, and thus (like position five) the way in which things are likely soon to manifest. Perhaps a change of attitude is called for now.

**8 Others' influence:** Sometimes called the environment card, because it is about how we interact with others and what we take from them, this card indicates the kind of input others have had with regard to the current situation. Sometimes this is not so obvious, as there is often no direct involvement by others, but think about how much we are influenced by others' thoughts and opinions – even if they are only something we have read in a newspaper! Sometimes this card can show in what way the environment – the world out there – is helping or obstructing our progress.

**9 Hopes and fears:** As its name suggests, this card indicates the individual's attitude towards how things are working out at present. Are we merely wishing for the best? Overcome with anxiety? Or are our hopes and fears moderate?

**10 The outcome:** This is the card to which everything else has been leading: the likely and best possible outcome. In a reading where a specific question has been asked, the card here will serve as the answer. In most cases, however, it describes a more general situation, one to which matters in the present seem to point.

## How the cards relate to each other
These positions will soon become second nature to you – and the more spreads you do, the sooner you will get to know them. In the mean time, take things slowly and get a feel for the way in which the cards all relate to one another – this requires some practice. The Celtic Cross can be viewed as made up of two components: the cross on the left and the pillar on the right. The right-hand column positions can be seen to

follow an upward line towards the future, culminating in the outcome in position ten. The left-hand cross positions are more or less centred in the present.

For now, experiment for yourself with this spread. You can consult the card interpretations in chapters four to eight of this book. You could, for instance, form a question not related to the unknown future but about your present overall circumstances. For example, 'What do the cards have to say about my life right now?' This way, you will be putting the Tarot itself to the test, for you will already know the answer. However, don't be in too much of a hurry to dismiss cards you don't like or don't agree with – remember that none of us wholly knows ourself! Above all, be serious and sincere with your question and honest with yourself when the answer arrives in the cards.

## The Horseshoe spread

The next spread we will look at uses only seven cards. As the name implies, it is based on the shape of a horseshoe, a traditional symbol of good luck in magical lore. If the Celtic Cross is formed from the standard decimal ten, the Horseshoe is made from the mystical seven. Perhaps this is the reason why the Horseshoe is associated with traditional fortune-telling, in which specific, detailed answers are preferred. You may choose to employ this spread for a briefer, more concise reading, but do still try to get a synthesis of all seven cards.

Supposing your specific question is, 'When will I meet a partner?', don't simply concentrate on the last card; see what the others are saying about your past up until now, what you are doing presently to bring a partnership about, and what might be standing in your way, such as an attitude of yours. Consider position four especially carefully;

it offers advice on the most appropriate way of obtaining your goal.

Shuffle the cards in the usual way, and then choose seven at random from the pack. The first card you choose goes in position one, the second in position two, and so on.

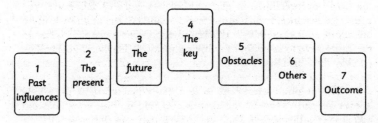

**1 Past influences:** This card describes a situation from the past that, as ever, may or may not be affecting the current situation. Don't think of the past literally as something that has passed, however. You may be overlooking some vital information.

**2 The present:** This position refers to conditions in the here and now, which in some cases you may want to change.

**3 The future:** This is the set of circumstances (on either the inner or the outer level) that you may end up in if nothing is done to change the present.

**4 The key:** Appearing as it does at the fulcrum of the spread, this card is the one that everything hinges on. It describes the probable best method or correct attitude to follow in order to achieve our aim. It is the key to success.

**5 Obstacles:** This card refers to conditions (on an inner or an outer level) that are standing in the way of progress. It also speaks of how we are coming to terms with a particular problem. If a beneficial card lands here, we can hardly consider it an obstacle, and it will act like a positive crossing card in the Celtic Cross – something that generates or contributes to the present.

**6 Others:** The card appearing in this position reveals the kind of influences and attitudes others bring to bear on the situation, for good or ill. But the extent to which others can influence our personal circumstances has much to do with ourselves.

**7 Outcome:** The card falling in this position indicates the probable resolution of the matter, or the answer to the question. It represents the kind of circumstances that will result from the outworkings of the present.

## The Horoscope spread

This circular spread is better suited to more comprehensive issues, where the answer may need to come from different angles. That is, it can be a divinatory source regarding various areas of our lives (our family, relationships, friends and finances) that can then be synthesised in a meaningful way. This spread reproduces the twelve houses of the astrological birth chart, with position one at nine o'clock, on the left. It then proceeds counter-clockwise around to position twelve.

Here, then, is an entire representation of the 'houses' of our life. However, I must stress again that what is before us in our outer lives, as mirrored in any spread, is largely self-created. In spiritual or occult studies such as Tarot, astrology and magic there's no avoiding personal responsibility. This is the teaching at the core of these subjects – we are co-creators in our universe, and what happens to us in our lives is, in the long run, no one else's fault!

The clever thing about this spread is that if we have a question to ask about a particular area of life, let's say romance, we need only consult the position specifically related to romance. But, of course, a love affair – depending on our personal circumstance – can be affected by various other factors, so we might want to study the cards falling in positions related to, say, money, communication, friends or even the past. Likewise, if the question is about money, we will also want to see which cards turn up in the positions for career and work. If you do choose to refer only to one 'house' position in search of your answer, however, you are quite entitled – indeed I would advise this – to overlay more cards in the same position, say three more. This will deepen your reading as you see what additional influences are at work. It is then up to you to combine these cards in a relevant way. Look for connections and relationships in the spread – these may not always be immediately obvious. Let the symbols speak to you.

To get started, shuffle the cards thoroughly in the usual way, select twelve for your face-down pile, and, from the bottom, place them in a circle moving counter-clockwise.

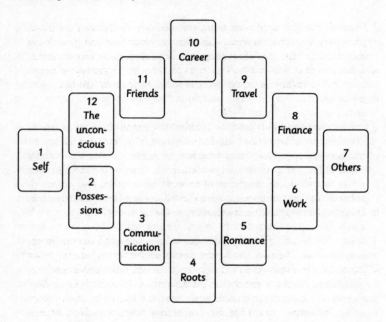

1 Self: The card falling here relates to our present circumstances and what we are doing to create them – in other words, what we are putting out into the world. It can refer to conditions surrounding our general vitality, and to our outer, ego personality. It quite often represents how others see us, for it also represents the persona, or the outer mask we adopt in society.

**2 Possessions:** The card occupying this position describes conditions surrounding personal finance, the way in which we are generating resources, and the possible obstacles or benefits to our material situation. It thus relates to all matters to do with monetary security: spending and saving money, possessions and how much we have – or don't have.

**3 Communication:** This position is about the manifold ways in which we communicate with the world around us. It reflects our ability to think, analyse and articulate, whether or not we are a convincing speaker, skilled at getting our point across. The card found in this position describes the mental resources available to us; our power to choose, decide and discriminate; our intellectual talents; and our wit, humour and cleverness (or the reverse, as the case may be!).

**4 Roots:** The card falling here relates to conditions in our intimate, personal world – usually the home, family and domestic scenery. But it's also about what is deep within us – our roots, what drives us from way back and how our family has influenced us. Like the base card of the Celtic Cross, it can describe what is at the source of the present situation, perhaps even what we are hiding from ourselves. Hence there is a metaphorical root (inner feelings) and a more literal one (parental influences); either or both may be having an important impact on the present.

**5 Romance:** ... and all that relates to joy, creativity, self-expression and the pleasure of the moment. This card indicates conditions obtaining for romance, along with our capacity for leisure and simple enjoyment.

It is essentially concerned with the energy of creation, with how we generate love for life in its deepest (though also simplest) sense – for what we give out, we get back. Essentially, this position pertains to matters of fun, entertainment and love life, and the card that falls here indicates whether or not we are having much fulfilment in these areas!

**6 Work:** This position covers work and industry in the broadest sense. It is chiefly concerned with the kind of effort we have to make to keep mind and body (and our routine, outer lives) properly maintained and in good working order. It is therefore about both the work we have to do on ourselves (diet, exercise) and the job we may go to each day. The card falling here not only describes present trends and conditions surrounding not only work (i.e. our day job) but can also give clues to what might be happening within the mind-body system – our psychological and physical health, general fitness and the like.

**7 Others:** The opposite of position One (as can be seen in the layout), this position is about the influence of partners, friends, neighbours and others generally. In essence it refers to conditions in our world that have been created through personal relationships; whether these are favourable or otherwise is suggested by the card that appears here. But do remember that what is being described here is generated, ultimately, by ourselves. Use this position in conjunction with position five.

**8 Finance:** This position is concerned specifically with matters to do with financial institutions: banks, building societies, the Inland Revenue, joint business ventures. It speaks of how we generate money through co-operation with others, and also the kinds of monetary obligations we have to other individuals or organisations (bills we have to pay). The card occupying this position describes the conditions surrounding our general financial health and liquidity; it speaks of how we stand here and may indicate whether the bank will look kindly upon us when we seek that loan!

**9 Travel:** This position relates mainly to long-distance travel that widens our horizons – hence foreign countries, whether for business or pleasure – although other kinds of getting about are also implied. A card falling here describes the present conditions surrounding any major journey we are taking or about to take. This journey may also be an intellectual or spiritual one. Thus this position can prove apposite if we are involved with further education, new philosophies, religious ideas and even politics. It is also concerned with how society functions from the moral standpoint, and so is the position to consult for conditions relating to legal matters.

**10 Career:** The card appearing in this position indicates what is happening with regard to our professional life. Whether we are the boss or the employee, it will tell us about possible changes within our existing career structure or new developments elsewhere. It often shows our short-term ambitions and their feasibility, as well as whether or not anything is yet materialising.

**11 Friends:** This position speaks of our casual acquaintances and associates, and also (together with position seven) gives information about our general social life and the way in which it is working out, positively or otherwise. The card occupying this position can show whether or not we are popular with our peers and describes our current capacity for co-operation with others, together with what we may or may not be getting from such associations.

**12 The unconscious:** Similar in meaning to positions number six and four in the Celtic Cross, this card shows not only what is part of our past experience, but also what may be hidden in the unconscious, playing an obscure (though perhaps powerful) role in the present situation. When using a Horoscope spread, we should pay great attention to this position, for the card occupying it can indicate conditions or energies (either subjective or objective) of which we have been largely unaware – and this can work against us. If the card here is obviously 'negative', then a little self-analysis may reveal the extent to which, say, we have recently been working against ourselves or how we have been putting harmful energies out into the world. Remember that the inner world creates the outer one. On the other hand, if a nice 'positive' card appears here, the Tarot may be calling our attention to how much we have overlooked the good in a current situation, burying the positive energy here in the unconscious. Perhaps, in this instance, we have been unable to see any special value or worth attached to a particular circumstance and we may need to count our blessings. The general idea with this position is that it contains energies that work behind the scenes (just as in this spread position twelve is just behind position one). The extent to which we are unaware of these energies, is the extent to which we may end up being our own worst enemy.

# Example readings

The following readings are two actual case histories from my files. I always jot down the spread positions when clients arrive for a consultation, and make brief notes of the reading when they have left. If you take this tip, you will be able to build up a picture of just how Tarot readings really work – having the theory is one thing, but you need to see precisely how it translates into practice. In these case histories, the changing circumstances of the querents were mirrored by the readings they had when they consulted me.

## Graham's reading

Graham was 33 years old when he consulted me, and in the first stages of a new love relationship, only months after seeing his ten-year marriage break up. At first, he had not accepted the end of his marriage, although it did not, in fact, take long for him to get his life back together. This new affair was something of a typical rebound relationship. Graham was insistent on simply getting on with his life, which, naturally, must include a girlfriend. He had been observing a woman called Jane for a little while in a local pub, planning just when to 'move in', as he put it. Graham, it should also be noted, is a successful, self-employed businessman who enjoys being in control of things, certainly his own life and quite often other people's! When he began going out with (and soon living with) Jane, he was gratified to feel that here was another successful 'move' that helped to perpetuate his self-image of the powerful, self-made person. And Jane was certainly, at ten years his junior, a boost for his ego.

Graham came to me for confirmation that the new relationship was going to turn out well. Little did he suspect that within a space of about four months things were to take an unexpected turn. I used the Celtic Cross spread.

 1 **The significator:** Ace of Cups
 2 **The crossing card:** King of Pentacles
 3 **The crown:** Nine of Pentacles
 4 **The base of the matter:** the Tower
 5 **The near future:** Knight of Wands
 6 **The recent past:** Judgement
 7 **Your influence:** Two of Swords
 8 **Others' influence:** Two of Cups
 9 **Hopes and fears:** Ace of Swords
 10 **The outcome:** Seven of Cups

**Card one:** Card one appeared in an almost text-book way. The Ace of Cups relates to new love life and the emergence of feelings sometimes hitherto undiscovered. Graham was indeed enjoying such emotional benefits at the time of the consultation.

**Card two:** The card that crossed the significator – the King of Pentacles – seemed to relate to qualities in Graham himself. In other words, Graham was able to bring about this new relationship by the sheer force of his personality. The crossing card (card two) is often what produces the significator. The King of Pentacles is, amongst other things, usually successful materially – Graham was in the high-earning bracket and there was little doubt that his chances of winning over Jane had been improved by his economic power.

**Card three:** As much was being said again in the crowning card, the Nine of Pentacles, which describes a sense of financial satisfaction.

**Card four:** But what might the Tower (card four – the base of the matter) mean? For one, it suggests a tense situation soon to arrive at boiling point (or already having done so). Apparently, however, no such tension existed at the time. (But I will return to this card later.)

**Card five:** For card five, the near future, Graham chose the Knight of Wands, which in this case pertained to something about Graham on an inner level as well as on the level of outer circumstance. Although successful in his work, he was – after ten years doing the same job – itching for a change of scene. The Knight of Wands invariably refers to a state of restlessness – the need for new horizons and fresh fields. But this position relates to future conditions too, remember.

**Card six:** The next card, Judgement, in the position of recent past, seemed to describe Graham's attitude to the marriage that had atrophied. He had, it seemed, thoroughly accepted that it was over for good; a chapter had been closed and he felt free to move on. Judgement generally indicates something finally coming to light. In this case it referred to Graham's discovery around this time that his ex-wife had a new boyfriend. This put the final nail in the coffin. With a new girlfriend of his own to occupy his emotions it was time to think ahead.

**Card seven:** However, the presence of the Two of Swords in position seven, indicating Graham's conscious or unconscious input into the situation, suggested that all was not as straightforward as it seemed. The Two of Swords often indicates that we are shying away from a conflict of some kind, letting sleeping dogs lie lest we upset the status quo. This conflict, I might add, did not involve Graham's ex-wife, and

I was unable to extract any clue from Graham himself as to what the tension implied in this card might be.

**Card eight:** The card relating to the influence of others, the Two of Cups, seemed to put us back on firmer ground, suggesting the potential for creative relationships. The fact that Jane was contributing to making the relationship easy-going and happy was obvious.

**Card nine:** The hopes and fears card was the Ace of Swords, which possibly indicated that Graham feared discord and arguments with his new girlfriend.

**Card ten:** The final outcome card was the Seven of Cups, a card suggesting all manner of distraction and the need to make realistic, utterly practical choices. This is perhaps not the most positive card to end with, for it implies a situation in which we may be fooling ourselves. Indeed, with the added presence of the Tower, the Knight of Wands and the Two of Swords, I was not initially optimistic regarding this affair. It *looked* OK on the surface, but for me these cards revealed a profound uncertainty on the part of Graham that this relationship was going to last. It was, of course, an uncertainty that he couldn't admit to.

**What the future held:** As a matter of fact, the relationship did eventually fold only four months after the reading, and for this reason: Graham soon became bored with Jane when his eye alighted on Sonja, a far more exciting proposition. In terms of the reading, this made perfect sense. The Tower showed that the current relationship was in fact built on insecure foundations, erected in the heat of the moment. The impending restlessness and thirst for newness was there in the Knight of Wands, and the Two of Swords indicated that Graham really did have inner doubts that he had temporarily silenced, creating the typical stasis that arises from blindfolding oneself to inner realities. The Seven of Cups shows that Graham was deluding himself about his feelings towards Jane (he never really had any) and was ready to be distracted and enchanted anew – precisely what happened when he took up with Sonja. Like the King of Pentacles that represents him in this spread, the ambitious and resourceful Graham simply _had_ to succeed in this new conquest!

## Paul's reading

Paul came to me on the advice of his girlfriend, Alicia. His story illustrates just how a life can be turned around almost 180 degrees in a relatively short space of time. Such transformations are, of course, reflected in the Tarot. Again, I used the Celtic Cross spread.

Paul seemed be one of life's inveterate non-achievers. It wasn't for lack of intelligence, wit or education, just that the twenty-nine-year-old ex-physics student seemed happy enough spending his days with like-minded friends in a local café, smoking, drinking and doing the _Guardian_ crossword. The amiable Paul seemed destined for the easy though aimless existence of a semi-layabout at the time when his partner suggested that I 'do his cards'. Occasional (and fruitless) trips to the Job Centre, naturally at the insistence of Alicia, were the only blot on his day. Alicia told me (raising her eyebrows) that Paul was 'waiting for the right job to come along'. As for the Tarot, Paul didn't, 'believe in that kind of stuff', though he did nonetheless consent to the reading.

1 The significator: Four of Cups
2 The crossing card: Four of Wands
3 The crown: Seven of Cups
4 The base of the matter: the Emperor
5 The near future: Ace of Pentacles
6 The recent past: Four of Pentacles
7 Your influence: Wheel of Fortune
8 Others' influence: Ace of Wands
9 Hopes and fears: Eight of Wands
10 The outcome: the Empress

**Card one:** The Four of Cups depicted Paul's existence at the time of the reading – one of unremarkable and minor pleasures, somewhat tinged with boredom though certainly not difficult or depressing.

**Card two:** The crossing card was the Four of Wands. As we noted in Chapter Five, this card is about material satisfaction from the success of our initiatives. Either Paul was satisfied with very little, or the ongoing security suggested by this card was producing the vague dissatisfaction and boredom of the Four of Cups. Either way, both of these Fours suggest stability and things simply remaining the same.

**Card three:** The Seven of Cups appeared as the crown, the card of unrealised potential. With this card we are faced with various attractive alternatives, though none of them necessarily realistic. It may have referred to Paul's apparent inability to secure regular employment (or perhaps his avoidance of it, as he waited for the right job). In my experience, the Seven of Cups always appears in self-deluding situations and, as we shall see, Paul was, in fact, kidding himself with the idea that he could perpetuate the role of the work-shy, armchair philosopher in the local coffee bar.

**Card four:** The base of the matter was the Emperor. This card symbolises the father role, that of the responsible authority figure who has learned to stand on their own two feet. You will realise at once that this hardly describes anything in Paul's life at the time of the reading – however, I shall return to this card later.

**Card five:** In the position of the near future was the Ace of Pentacles. This looks like a good augur: the forthcoming availability of new financial resources. But this card, like the Emperor, had me baffled – responsibility and the earning of money didn't seem to be Paul's forte. Nevertheless I did mention to him that financial improvements seemed to be on their way, though I was at a loss to think of how.

**Card six:** In the position of the recent past, we find the Four of Pentacles, a reference to the need for economic caution – but this is also, significantly, the third Four card: once more, stability and security.

**Card seven:** If cards four and six did not seem to fit Paul's present reality, then neither did the Wheel of Fortune, especially in a position pertaining to how we have influenced the present or forthcoming situation. Remember the two initial (and more appropriate) cards suggesting stasis and no change! The standard interpretation of the Wheel is irrevocable change and transformation, as a result of which we begin a completely new chapter in our life – which didn't seem a likely option under the present conditions. I asked Paul what plans he had for the near future and received only a vague shrug and mutterings about getting a good job.

**Card eight:** The Ace of Wands in the position of others' influence seems to refer to the encouragement of Alicia – she was the dynamic force behind him, helping to bring about this change of circumstance.

**Card nine:** The Eight of Wands in the position of hopes and fears is a card of swiftness, movement and progress after delays. Perhaps Paul felt that everything was happening too quickly for his liking, but there was no doubt of the eventual appropriateness of all these changes.

**Card ten:** Finally, we arrive at the Outcome card, the Empress, which is not only indicative of material well-being, new life and growth in Paul's life but also presaged an impending new role.

**What the future held:** Let's now jump ahead two months, which is when I heard that Paul had finally got a job. When I saw him a month after that, I learned with amazement that he'd quickly been promoted to a managerial position with, of course, an increased salary. He now had plans to buy a house with Alicia – plans which eventually materialised. What's more, Paul was indeed looking forward to a new role – as a father. Alicia announced her pregnancy shortly after Paul's promotion, which was some four months after the initial reading.

We can see in retrospect the degree to which Paul was on the cusp of huge changes, which he had unconsciously engineered himself. This is important to remember. With the Emperor card in the base of the matter, Paul was more than ready to do something practical with his life. Although outwardly he was merely going with the flow, it would seem that he had considerable ambition gestating deep inside, and when the chance came to get his life together materially, he pounced on it. The effects of the Wheel of Fortune – the new job, the mortgage, parenthood – did not just happen to him; he got what he had wanted all along, once the time was right. In retrospect it was obvious that cards eight and nine supplied much of Paul's energy. And that is often the way the most significant things happen in our lives; there is usually a sense that our time has come, but the dynamics for major change are already there within us. It should be no surprise to find that they are echoed in the cards.

## Tips for reading the cards

1 Always be sincere with your question.
2 Don't be in a hurry to 'get' the meaning of whatever cards appear.
3 Avoid pat interpretations; always try go deeper and understand fully.
4 Try to absorb the symbolism and make wider lateral connections.
5 The cards will not necessarily refer to something external and objective but may perhaps say something about your mental or emotional make-up.
6 Don't insist on a curt 'yes' or 'no'; if the answer seems rather elliptical, ask yourself what the Tarot is really trying to say to you.
7 Don't expect the cards to foretell future events as if you or the person you are reading for had nothing to do with them.
8 When reading for yourself, don't try to simply disregard the 'negative' cards – they may have something to teach you. Self-honesty is paramount!

9  When reading for others, remember that the person is more important than the cards! Whatever cards turn up, don't try to force their text-book meanings on the person's life – find out what real situation (physical, spiritual or emotional) the cards may be reflecting.

10  If your querent has a run of 'negative' cards, try to find out in a sympathetic way what possible crisis may be present, and reassure them that the cards do not mean anything negative is fated to happen.

# Afterword

As we have seen, the Tarot can be used for a variety of purposes, and readings can be classified into certain types. There are those that help us to gain an overall perspective on our lives during any given period, there are those that seek to divine by looking at our present situation in terms of conscious and unconscious, and there are those that look for 'objective' answers to specific questions. The first is what we might call a general reading, the second is more psychological and in-depth, and the third is geared towards a direct response.

In practice, however, readings can be a combination of all three approaches. What it is vital to remember – and certainly when reading for others – is that the individual person comes first. In any consultation, the cards should be used as a kind of interface between what is happening in the person's life and the kind of person they are – in other words, to reveal some kind of connection between who they are and what has manifested in their lives. This consideration is extremely important – for what you are is what you will attract.

Many of the readings I have done for clients have entailed relationship matters, quite often involving people who are not fully satisfied with their lot and sometimes even considering extra-marital affairs. These people wanted the cards to tell them that something new and wonderful was going to come along to relieve their boredom. But it became plain to me that such an individual was going to be dissatisfied with whoever they encountered. Their whole attitude to life was 'What will I get out of it?' and it had never occurred to them that perhaps they ought to put something into life first. In other words, they remained blind to their own failings.

Remember, the ultimate message of symbolic divinatory systems like the Tarot is the same as that found in ancient Delphi: 'know thyself'. That means not only get to know your own real needs, values and limitations but also get to know the effect you are having on those around you. What are your real strengths and innate talents? What is your capacity to form meaningful and happy relationships? What are your natural gifts? On the other side of the coin, what requires great effort on your part that some people seem to find easy? All in all, why do events manifest in your life the way they do? We might also remember the saying from Shakespeare: 'to thine own self be true'. Such a requirement is never more urgent than when reading the Tarot. Get into the habit of asking just why each card has appeared in your spread at any one time – and remember, sincere pondering on the question is always more valuable than a quick answer.

I hope that this introductory guide to Tarot divination will inspire you to use the Tarot as a means to understanding yourself and your friends, and to help you make everyday decisions. You may even want to pursue your studies further. Of course, each individual will make their own relationship to the cards over a period of time, and each person tends to interpret them slightly differently. Indeed, the Tarot is quite democratic in this way, and this is just as it should be. As long as we arrive at the correct destination – a place where we are perhaps a little wiser, where we are better for having understood, then the route we take is largely unimportant. Learning the Tarot may be far easier than you first thought, because letting the images speak to you is quite simple if you are prepared to listen, and listen well.

# Further Reading

Some of the titles listed below are now considered standard Tarot texts. Those marked with an asterisk are particularly recommended for beginners.

Annett, Sally and Shepherd, Rowena, *The Atavist Tarot,* W. Foulsham & Co. Ltd, 2003

Bellenghi, Allesandro, *Cartomancy,* Ebury Press, 1988

Blofeld, John, *I Ching: The Book of Change,* Mandala, 1984

*Bunker, Dusty, *Numerology, Astrology and Dreams,* Whitford Press, 1987

Butler, Bill, *The Definitive Tarot,* Century, 1975

Campbell, Joseph & Roberts, Richard, *Tarot Revelations,* Vernal Equinox, 1987

*Donaldson, Terry, *Principles of Tarot,* Thorsons, 1996

*Douglas, Alfred, *The Tarot,* Penguin Books, 1972

Eason, Cassandra, *Tarot Talks to the Woman Within,* W. Foulsham & Co. Ltd, 2002

Giles, Cynthia, *Tarot: The Complete Guide,* Hale, 1993

Greene, Liz & Sharman-Burke, Juliet, *The Mythic Tarot,* Century Hutchinson, 1986

*Herbin Evelyn, *Way of Tarot,* Thorsons, 2001

*Ozaniec, Naomi, *The Illustrated Guide to The Tarot,* Godsfield, 1999

*Ozaniec, Naomi, *Tarot,* Teach Yourself Books, 1998

## Further Reading

*Mann, A.T., *The Elements of Tarot,* Element Books
*Pollack, Rachel, *Seventy Eight Degrees of Wisdom, Part One: The Major Arcana,* Aquarian Press, 1980
*Pollack, Rachel, *Seventy Eight Degrees of Wisdom, Part Two: The Minor Arcana,* Aquarian Press, 1983
Pollack, Rachel, *The New Tarot,* Aquarian Press, 1989
McCormack, Kathleen, *The Illustrated Guide To The Tarot,* Aurum, 1998
*Sharman-Burke, Juliet, *Understanding the Tarot: A Personal Teaching Guide,* Rider, 1998
Waite, A.E., *The Pictorial Key to the Tarot,* Rider, London 1971
Willis, Tony, *Magick and the Tarot,* Aquarian Press, 1988

# Index

# Index